Chapter 1:
Breakfast
5

NEW Edition
Personal
Points™

Chapter 2:
Lunch
26

Chapter 3:
Dinner
46

Keep it healthy. Keep it simple.

We understand that preparing healthy meals is only one component of your busy life, so we're offering this collection of 5-ingredient 15-minute recipes to help you get breakfast, lunch, or dinner on the table with ease. The recipes call for five ingredients or fewer (excluding water, oil, cooking spray, salt, and pepper), or they take 15 minutes or less to prepare; many of the recipes meet both criteria. With these simple recipes, you can spend less time grocery shopping, more little time cooking, and more time enjoying meals with family and friends.

Chapter 4:
Soup
66

WeightWatchers

Introduction

Weight Watchers is the world's top science-based plan for weight loss, but the program is not just about the numbers on the scale. Our approach emphasizes balance in what you eat and in a lifestyle built around joy, connection, and the power of healthy habits. Instead of following someone else's definition of healthy, WW allows you to discover your own.

You'll eat what you love.

Everything is on the menu! The myWW+ program gives you the freedom to make choices that work for how you eat. You'll have delicious meals, discover new favorites, and feel good about your eating habits while successfully losing weight!

You'll find what moves you.

The activity comes naturally when you enjoy what you're doing. Maybe you're already committed to a sport or exercise routine, or perhaps the Weight Watchers community will help you find a new approach. Either way, the goal is to feel stronger, more powerful, and proud of what your body can do.

You'll shift your mindset

Weight Watchers emphasizes thinking in new ways and confronting challenging moments with self-compassion. You can turn to your fellow members for support and encouragement in real life and online.

You'll benefit from the power of PersonalPoints®

You'll benefit from the power of PersonalPoints®.
Science-backed and easy to use, the SmartPoints system guides you to a healthier eating pattern. Members learn the specifics about how to calculate PersonalPoints from their WW Coaches, but here are some basics:
• Every food and drink has a PersonalPoints value based on calories, saturated fat, sugar, and protein.
• You get a daily PersonalPoints Budget to spend on any food or drink you like.
• You'll keep track of your PersonalPoints in the WW app.
• We know that no two days are the same, so on a day that you do not use all your daily PersonalPoints, up to four of those PersonalPoints will rollover. You don't have to do anything-the WW app will keep track of it for you!

For more flexibility, you have ZeroPoint™ foods.

On myWW+, you'll get a customized list of foods that you don't have to measure or count. These foods we want to guide you to eat more often because they form the foundation of a healthy eating pattern, and you have a low risk of overeating them.

What's your plan?

When it comes to losing weight and getting healthier, WW knows that what works for one person might not work for another. The answer? Three science-backed, proven plans tailored to fit individual needs and personal preferences. We've developed every recipe in this book to work for all programs, and we've given the SmartPoints values upfront for each.

Find recipes that fit.

Every recipe includes SmartPoints values for all three Weight Watchers plans, so choosing the meals that fit best with your SmartPoints Budget is easy. As you look at the recipe chapters, you can see what recipes work best for you-you'll even find recipes with just 1 or 2 SmartPoints per serving.

PersonalPoints vs. SmartPoints: What's Changed?

SmartPoints uses a similar foundation of accumulating points and then using them on specific foods. With PersonalPoints, there is a step toward something more focused on each aspect of a person's routine, including exercise.

This uses a cutting-edge algorithm to break down what a person has to eat and what should be used for their point allotment.

What is the new WW program

PersonalPoints™ brings together three groundbreaking innovations - a personalized ZeroPoint™ foods list, a Points® algorithm that makes healthy choices simpler, and rewards for building healthy habits - to provide a customized path to weight loss. And "personalized" isn't just a buzzword - it's scientifically proven that individualized TH approaches lead to more significant weight loss than a one-size-fits-all approach!

What can I eat on WW?

Anything—seriously. Nothing is off-limits! Our PersonalPoints Engine will determine your unique PersonalPoints Budget and individualized ZeroPoint foods list when you join WW. You can eat whatever you want—follow your Budget!—and reach for ZeroPoint foods as often as you like, without spending any Points.

How are PersonalPoint different from SmartPoints?

Let us count the exciting ways! Our brand-new algorithm crunches even more nutritional data, so you're guided toward the healthiest choices. Foods higher in fiber and healthy fats like avocados, almonds, and some whole grains are now lower in Points. We're also nudging you away from added sugars and unhealthy fats. Some foods may have gone up a bit in Points, but our science makes sure you still have plenty in your Budget for the foods you love.

Why can't I stay on Green/Blue/Purple? I want to keep my old ZeroPoint foods!

Change can be tricky when things are going great, but you now get an entirely individualized plan and ZeroPoint foods list based on the foods you love—and more personalization leads to more success. Join WW, then tell us which foods those are via our PersonalPoints Engine—they'll most likely appear on your ZeroPoint foods list.

Do I have to count calories?

When it comes to nutrition, calories don't tell the whole story. PersonalPoints factor in calories, protein, and fiber differentiating between natural and added sugars and unsaturated versus saturated fats. Your Points Budget is one-of-a-kind and will guide you toward a healthier eating pattern so you'll lose weight and feel good. Just eat, track Points, and lose weight.

Chapter 1:
Breakfast

Grilled Breakfast Kebabs with Honey Mustard Dipping Sauce

Total Time: 0:25 **Prep:** 0:15 **Cook:** 0:10 **Serves:** 4 **Difficulty:** Easy

If you're looking for a way to make breakfast more fun, look no further than this recipe. Chunks of breakfast sausage are threaded with vegetables for morning-meal kebabs that get dunked into a creamy honey mustard sauce. If you have trouble finding turkey breakfast sausage in your supermarket, look in the freezer section near the other breakfast items.

Ingredients

Cooking spray — 0
4 spray(s)

Plain fat free Greek yogurt — 0
½ cup(s)

Mustard — 0
2 Tbsp, yellow-variety

Honey — 5
1 Tbsp

Chives — 0
2 tsp, chopped

Cayenne pepper — 0
1 pinch(es), or to taste

Mild breakfast links turkey sausage — 11
8 oz, cut in bite-size pieces

Fresh mushroom(s) — 0
24 medium, cremini-variety

Fresh cherry tomato(es) — 0
24 medium

Fresh parsley — 0
2 Tbsp, chopped (optional)

Instructions

1 If using wooden skewers, soak them in water for 30 minutes. Coat a grill rack with cooking spray. Close the grill lid, and heat the grill to medium-high (about 450°F).

2 In a small bowl, whisk together the yogurt, mustard, honey, chives, and cayenne pepper; set aside until ready to serve.

3 Onto 12 (8- to 10-inch) skewers, thread 2 sausage pieces, 2 mushrooms, and 2 tomatoes. Coat the kebabs with cooking spray. Arrange the kebabs on the grill rack. Close the grill lid and cook until grill marks appear and the kebabs are heated through, 3 to 4 minutes per side. Serve the kebabs with the sauce. Garnish with the parsley, if desired.

4 Serving size: 2 kebabs and about 2 ½ tbsp sauce

Copycat Egg & English muffin breakfast sandwiches

Total Time: 0:15   **Prep:** 0:10   **Cook:** 0:05   **Serves:** 2   **Difficulty:** Easy

Modeled after the classic drive-through breakfast favorite (you know the ones!), this easy fast food copycat recipe can put a healthier version on your plate in just 15 minutes. The key to nailing the copycat version is using a Mason jar lid to hold and steam the eggs into a perfectly round shape with perfectly moist texture. You'll want to use wide-mouth lids that measure 3 ½ inches in diameter.

Ingredients

Cooking spray 0
4 spray(s)

Egg(s) 0
2 large egg(s)

Table salt 0
2 pinch(es)

Black pepper 0
2 pinch(es)

Uncooked Canadian bacon 1
2 slice(s)

Light English muffin(s) 4
2 muffin(s), lightly toasted

Reduced fat American cheese 4
2 slice(s)

Instructions

1 Heat a large or medium skillet over medium-high heat. Coat 2 wide-mouth Mason jar lids (flat lids and sealing rings) with cooking spray and arrange in the skillet upside down so that they're like 2 shallow bowls. Crack 1 egg into each lid and pierce the yolk a few times with a paring knife. Sprinkle a pinch of salt and black pepper over each egg. Pour ⅔ cup water into the skillet, cover, and steam until the eggs are cooked through, 2 to 3 minutes.

2 Using tongs, remove the lids with eggs to a plate. Reduce the heat to medium, and discard any remaining water in the pan. Arrange the Canadian bacon in the pan; cook until lightly browned and heated through, 30 seconds to 1 minute on each side.

3 Turn the lids with eggs upside down and remove the lid ring; carefully pull off the flat lid. On the bottom of each English muffin, arrange 1 cheese slice, 1 egg, 1 Canadian bacon slice, and the top of the English muffin.

4 Serving size: 1 sandwich

Breakfast barley with kimchi & fried egg

Total Time: 0:12 **Prep:** 0:02 **Cook:** 0:10 **Serves:** 2 **Difficulty:** Easy

When we say, "Everything's on the menu," at WW, we should also add that everything's on the breakfast menu too. This grain bowl will wake up your palate with its tangy, probiotic-filled kimchi topping.

Ingredients

Cooking spray — 0
4 spray(s)

Unsalted butter — 6
1 Tbsp

Cooked pearl barley — 4
1 cup(s)

Low sodium soy sauce — 0
1 Tbsp

Kimchi — 0
½ cup(s), divided

Egg(s) — 0
2 large egg(s)

Uncooked scallion(s) — 0
1 medium, thinly sliced (optional)

Instructions

1. In a medium nonstick skillet, melt the butter over medium heat. Add the barley and soy sauce and cook until heated through, 2 to 3 minutes, stirring occasionally. Remove the pan from heat.

2. Finely chop half the kimchi. Stir the chopped kimchi into the barley. Divide the barley between 2 bowls.

3. Wipe out the skillet. Coat the skillet with cooking spray and heat on medium. Add the eggs and cook until the whites are set and the yolks are still runny or to desired doneness, 3 to 5 minutes.

4. Top each bowl of barley with 1 egg. Divide the remaining kimchi between the bowls. Top with the scallions (if using).

5. Serving size: 1 bowl

Jammy egg breakfast sandwich

Total Time: 0:20 **Prep:** 0:05 **Cook:** 0:15 **Serves:** 4 **Difficulty:** Easy

If you've never heard of jammy eggs, picture tender, perfectly cooked whites and gooey yolks that fall somewhere between runny and set. Not as messy as sunny-side up eggs but richer than hard-boiled ones, they're perfect for stuffing into a grab-and-go sandwich.

Ingredients

Egg(s) — 0
4 item(s), large

Light English muffin(s) — 8
4 muffin(s), split

Uncooked Canadian bacon — 3
4 slice(s)

Light cheddar cheese — 4
¾ cup(s), shredded

Uncooked scallion(s) — 0
6 Tbsp, chopped

Table salt — 0
¼ tsp

Black pepper — 0
¼ tsp

Instructions

1. Bring a large pot of water to a boil over high heat. Prepare a medium bowl of ice water. Add the eggs to the boiling water and cook for exactly 7 minutes. Using a slotted spoon, immediately transfer the eggs to the ice water and let cool for 1 minute. Gently crack and peel the eggs.

2. In a toaster oven or 350°F oven, toast the English muffins for 1 to 2 minutes. Place 1 slice of bacon on each muffin bottom. Sprinkle each muffin top with 3 tbsp of the cheese. Return the muffins to the oven and toast until the bacon is heated through and the cheese is melted, 2 to 3 minutes.

3. Using a sharp knife, slice the eggs in half. Top each slice of bacon with 2 egg halves. Sprinkle with the scallions, salt, and black pepper. Cover with the muffin tops, cheese-side down.

4. Serving size: 1 sandwich

Air-Fried Oatmeal Breakfast Bars

Total Time: 0:25   **Prep:** 0:10   **Cook:** 0:10   **Serves:** 4   **Difficulty:** Easy

If you're a fan of baked oatmeal but want something quicker and that makes a smaller batch, this recipe is for you. The oatmeal mixture (made with oat flour that you make in the blender, along with whole oats) is patted into a square and air-fried until it's crisp on top and chewy-hearty inside. The finishing touches are a swoop of yogurt and a fresh berry topping. Done in only 20 minutes, it's easy enough for a weekday.

Ingredients

Uncooked old fashioned rolled oats — 10
1 ½ cup(s), divided

Unsweetened applesauce — 0
½ cup(s)

Powdered peanut butter — 1
3 Tbsp

Honey — 3
2 tsp

Baking soda — 0
½ tsp

Table salt — 0
¼ tsp

Ground cinnamon — 0
¼ tsp

Plain fat free Greek yogurt — 0
¼ cup(s)

Fresh blueberries — 0
¼ cup(s)

Fresh blackberries — 0
¼ cup(s), chopped

Instructions

1 In a blender, process ¾ cup oats on high speed until a fine flour forms, 30 seconds to 1 minute. In a medium bowl, whisk together the applesauce, powdered peanut butter, honey, baking soda, salt, and cinnamon. Stir in the oat flour and the remaining oats. Onto a piece of parchment paper, pat the mixture into a 5 ½ x 4-inch rectangle.

2 Preheat an air fryer, if necessary, to 350°F. Using the parchment paper, lift the oatmeal mixture and place it (and the paper) in the air fryer basket. Air-fry until browned on top and cooked through, 10 to 12 minutes.

3 Remove from the air fryer and cut into 4 equal pieces. Cool slightly. Spread 1 tbsp yogurt over each oatmeal bar; sprinkle the berries evenly over the bars.

4 Serving size: 1 bar

Savory Italian Oatmeal Breakfast Bowl

Total Time: 0:20 **Prep:** 0:10 **Cook:** 0:10 **Serves:** 1 **Difficulty:** Easy

6

Good news for team savory breakfast: Your morning bowl of porridge doesn't have to be sweet. Oatmeal is a whole grain, after all, and can easily go in a savory direction the way that farro, quinoa, or freekeh can. Here, we stir a little Parmesan into cooked oats and top them with sautéed chicken sausage, grape tomatoes, spinach, and egg. We cook the oats in the microwave for hands-off convenience, and at reduced power to help prevent boil-overs. The recipe serves one and can easily be multiplied to serve more; just move the oatmeal cooking to a large-enough saucepan on the stove.

Ingredients

Cooking spray — 0
4 spray(s)

Uncooked old fashioned rolled oats — 3
½ cup(s)

Kosher salt — 0
⅛ tsp

Grated Parmesan cheese — 1
1 Tbsp, divided

Cooked chicken sausage(s) — 2
1 ½ oz, chopped

Grape tomatoes — 0
4 item(s), halved

Fresh baby spinach — 0
1 cup(s)

Egg(s) — 0
1 large egg(s)

Instructions

1. Place the oats in a 4-cup glass measuring cup or a medium microwave-safe bowl. Stir in 1 cup water and salt. Microwave at 70% power until done, stirring occasionally, 4 to 5 minutes. Stir in 2 tsp cheese. Spoon the oats into a shallow bowl.

2. Meanwhile, coat a small nonstick skillet with cooking spray. Heat the pan over medium. Add the sausage and tomatoes; cook, stirring occasionally, until the sausage browns and the tomatoes soften, 4 to 5 minutes. Add the spinach; cook, stirring constantly, until the spinach wilts, about 1 minute. Spoon the spinach mixture over the oats.

3. Off the heat, recoat the pan with cooking spray. Heat the pan over medium. Crack the egg into the pan; cook until the whites are set and the yolk is cooked to your desired degree of doneness, 2 to 3 minutes. Arrange the egg over the oatmeal. Sprinkle the remaining 1 tsp cheese over the top.

4. Serving size: 1 bowl

Veggie-Loaded Breakfast Flatbread

5

Total Time: 0:15   Prep: 0:10   Cook: 0:05   Serves: 1   Difficulty: Easy

Toasted pita flatbread offers a great way to pile on veggies and start your day off in a produce-packed way. A quick stint under the broiler crisps the pita so that it holds up well under the vegetables, which get lightly wilted in a skillet. A little feta cheese provides richness, and a fried egg provides protein. You can easily scale the recipe up to serve two or more people; just use larger skillets to cook a greater volume of vegetables and more eggs.

Ingredients

Cooking spray — 0
4 spray(s)

Whole wheat pita(s) — 4
1 large

Egg(s) — 0
1 large egg(s)

Kosher salt — 0
1/8 tsp, divided

Black pepper — 0
1/8 tsp, divided

Fresh baby spinach — 0
2 cup(s)

Uncooked zucchini — 0
1 cup(s), sliced, ribbons

Grape tomatoes — 0
1/4 cup(s), halved

Crumbled feta cheese — 1
1 Tbsp

Instructions

1. Preheat the broiler to High. Broil the pita until crisp, 1 to 2 minutes on each side.

2. Meanwhile, coat a small nonstick skillet with cooking spray. Heat the pan over medium heat. Crack the egg into the pan; sprinkle with a pinch each of salt and pepper. Cook until desired degree of doneness, 3 to 4 minutes.

3. While the egg cooks, coat a medium nonstick skillet with cooking spray. Heat the pan over medium-high heat. Add the spinach, zucchini, tomatoes, and remaining pinch each of salt and pepper; cook, tossing frequently with tongs, until just wilted, 1 to 2 minutes. Arrange the spinach mixture on the pita; sprinkle with feta and top with the egg.

4. Serving size: 1 topped flatbread

Butternut & Winter Greens Breakfast Rolls

Total Time: 0:45 **Prep:** 0:15 **Cook:** 0:25 **Serves:** 8 **Difficulty:** Easy

Take a break from sugary breakfast rolls with this savory riff featuring butternut squash, Swiss chard, and feta cheese. To keep prep easy, we use store-bought crescent roll dough, and we quickly cook the squash and greens together in the microwave. We also recommend buying pre-chopped squash; if the pieces are large, cut them to a smaller dice. To give the stuffed rolls plenty of room to expand, we cook them in a 9-inch cake pan. If you don't have one, you could use a 9-inch pie plate or a smaller 8-inch cake pan.

Ingredients

Cooking spray — 0
4 spray(s)

Uncooked butternut squash — 0
1 cup(s), diced

Uncooked Swiss chard — 0
5 cup(s), chopped

Reduced fat crescent roll dough — 28
8 oz

Kosher salt — 0
¼ tsp

Black pepper — 0
¼ tsp

Crumbled feta cheese — 12
⅔ cup(s)

Instructions

1. Preheat the oven to 375°F. Coat a 9-inch cake pan with cooking spray.

2. Place the butternut in a large microwave-safe bowl; top with the chard. Cover the bowl tightly with plastic wrap; pierce once with a knife to vent. Microwave on High for 4 minutes. Spread the squash mixture onto a plate lined with paper towels. Let stand 5 minutes to cool slightly.

3. Unroll the dough on a piece of wax or parchment paper and pinch all seams to seal; pat the dough into an even rectangular shape. Spread the butternut mixture evenly over the dough; sprinkle with the salt and pepper. Sprinkle the cheese evenly over the top. Starting at one long edge, roll up the dough jelly-roll fashion; pinch the seam to seal. Cut the dough crosswise into 8 equal slices. Arrange the slices, cut sides up, in the prepared pan.

4. Bake the rolls until puffed and golden brown, 20 to 22 minutes. Serve warm.

5. Serving size: 1 roll

Chicken-Sausage Breakfast Burger

Total Time: 0:25 Prep: 0:15 Cook: 0:10 Serves: 4 Difficulty: Easy

For a fun twist on the usual breakfast sandwich, try our easy breakfast burger. It starts with homemade sage-infused chicken sausage patties that are lean but stay moist thanks to a drizzle of olive oil. The jam-mustard combo brings a hint of sweetness if you're the kind of person who loves ketchup on their egg sandwiches. Make this and eat it right away or break it up into smaller steps for meal prepping. Make the jam mixture and cook the sausage patties, then store it all in the fridge. Each morning, reheat a sausage patty in the microwave (for 15 to 30 seconds), fry up or scramble an egg, and build your burger.

Ingredients

Ingredient	Points
Cooking spray — 4 spray(s)	0
98% fat-free uncooked ground chicken breast — 12 oz	0
Olive oil — 2 tsp	3
Ground sage — 1 tsp	0
Garlic powder — ½ tsp	0
Kosher salt — ⅝ tsp, divided	0
Black pepper — ⅝ tsp, divided	0
Egg(s) — 4 item(s), large	0
Reduced-sugar mixed berry jam — 2 Tbsp	3
Whole-grain mustard — 2 Tbsp	1
Light whole wheat hamburger buns — 4 bun(s)	8
Fresh baby spinach — 1⅓ cup(s)	0
Fresh tomato(es) — 4 slice(s)	0

Instructions

1. In a medium bowl, combine the chicken, oil, sage, garlic powder, and ½ tsp each salt and black pepper. Coat a large nonstick skillet with cooking spray; heat the pan over medium. Divide the chicken mixture into 4 equal portions (it will be soft). Gently shape each into a ball and add to the heated pan; flatten with a spatula. Cook until browned and cooked through, about 3 minutes per side. Remove the patties from the pan.

2. Off the heat, recoat the pan with cooking spray. Heat the pan over medium-low. Crack the eggs into the pan and sprinkle evenly with the remaining ⅛ tsp each salt and black pepper. Cook until the whites are set, about 3 minutes, or to desired degree of doneness.

3. In a small bowl, stir together the jam and mustard. Spread the jam mixture evenly over the top half of each bun. Layer the bottom half of each bun with ⅓ cup spinach, 1 tomato slice, 1 patty, and 1 egg.

4. Serving size: 1 burger

Apple-Cinnamon Oatmeal Breakfast Bread

Total Time: 0:35 **Prep:** 0:10 **Cook:** 0:20 **Serves:** 4 **Difficulty:** Easy

Creative easy breakfast ideas don't get much simpler. Use WW oatmeal cups as the base for these individual breakfast breads. They're made in mini loaf pans and come together in minutes. They're great hot but delicious at room temperature, too. Enjoy at home or toss into a container for breakfast on-the-go.

Ingredients

Cooking spray — 0
2 spray(s)

WW Apple Cinnamon Instant Oatmeal — 6
2 container(s)

White self-rising flour — 4
⅓ cup(s)

Egg(s) — 0
1 large egg(s)

Fresh apple(s) — 0
1 large, Fuji suggested, grated on large holes of a box grater

Fat free skim milk — 1
¼ cup(s)

Crystallized ginger — 1
1 ½ Tbsp, finely chopped

Instructions

1. Preheat oven to 350°F. Coat 4 mini loaf pans with cooking spray.

2. Place oatmeal in a bowl; sift flour over top. Whisk egg with milk in another bowl; stir into oat mixture. Add apple; stir to combine. Divide among prepared pans; smooth in an even layer and sprinkle with ginger.

3. Bake until a tester inserted in center of a loaf comes out clean, 20-25 minutes.

4. Let cool slightly in pan before removing.

5. Serving size: 1 loaf

Blueberry-Banana Oatmeal Breakfast Bread

3

Total Time: 0:35   Prep: 0:10   Cook: 0:20   Serves: 4   Difficulty: Easy

WW oatmeal cups can be turned into quick, easy, adorable breakfast cakes using mini loaf pans. Enjoy these 5-ingredient breads for breakfast, snack or dessert. The varieties are endless - add in any fresh or frozen unsweetened fruit you have on hand. If you don't have mini loaf pans, you can also use mini muffin pans.

Ingredients

Cooking spray — 0
2 spray(s)

WW Maple Brown Sugar Instant Oatmeal — 6
2 container(s)

White self-rising flour — 4
⅓ cup(s)

Egg(s) — 0
1 large egg(s)

Fat free skim milk — 1
¼ cup(s)

Banana(s) — 0
1 medium, ripe, mashed with a fork

Unsweetened frozen blueberries — 0
½ cup(s), or fresh blueberries

Powdered sugar (confectioner's) — 1
1 tsp

Instructions

1. Preheat oven to 350°F. Coat 4 mini loaf pans with cooking spray.

2. Place oatmeal in a bowl; sift flour over top. Whisk egg with milk in another bowl; stir into oat mixture. Add banana and blueberries; stir to combine. Divide among prepared pans; smooth in an even layer.

3. Bake until a tester inserted in center of a loaf comes out clean, 20-25 minutes.

4. Let cool slightly in pan; remove and serve sprinkled with powdered sugar.

5. Serving size: 1 loaf

Sweet Potato Breakfast Bowl 6

Total Time: 0:15   **Prep:** 0:05   **Cook:** 0:10   **Serves:** 1   **Difficulty:** Easy

This meal comes together in a snap, and the smaller you chop the ingredients, the faster it cooks. Make it your own by adding your favorite fresh herbs.

Ingredients

Cooking spray — 0
4 spray(s)

Uncooked onion(s) — 0
½ cup(s), chopped

Uncooked sweet Italian turkey sausage — 3
3 oz, or other flavor

Fresh mushroom(s) — 0
½ cup(s), chopped

Cooked sweet potato(es) — 2
½ cup(s), diced

Olive oil — 1
1 tsp, used to roast potatoes

Egg(s) — 0
2 large egg(s)

Instructions

1 Coat a large nonstick skillet with cooking spray. Heat over medium heat. Add onion and cook, stirring frequently, until soft, 3 to 4 minutes. Add sausage, and cook, breaking up any large pieces with a wooden spoon, until cooked through and starting to brown, about 2 to 3 minutes. Add mushrooms and cook, stirring frequently, until soft, another 2 to 3 minutes. Stir in sweet potatoes and cook until warm. Transfer to a serving bowl and cover to keep warm.

2 Wipe out skillet and off heat, recoat with cooking spray. Place skillet over medium heat. Add eggs and cook until whites start to set, about 2 minutes (or longer, if desired). Flip eggs and let cook for 10 seconds more. Place eggs over sweet potato mixture and serve immediately.

3 Serving size: 1 breakfast bowl

Cherry-spice oatmeal breakfast bread

Total Time: 0:35   **Prep:** 0:10   **Cook:** 0:20   **Serves:** 4   **Difficulty:** Easy

Fresh cherries add wonderful sweetness, color and moisture to these 5-ingredient breakfast cakes. They take less than 10 minutes to prepare and are a tasty change of pace from eating oatmeal. When fresh cherries are not in season, swap in frozen ones. You can also personalize these cute mini breads with your favorite fruit, oat or almond milk, and other flavor WW oatmeal cups.

Ingredients

Cooking spray — 0
2 spray(s)

WW Apple Cinnamon Instant Oatmeal — 6
2 container(s)

White self-rising flour — 4
⅓ cup(s)

Egg(s) — 0
1 large egg(s)

Fat free skim milk — 1
¼ cup(s)

Cherries — 0
1 cup(s), pitted, roughly chopped

Powdered sugar (confectioner's) — 1
2 tsp

Instructions

1. Preheat oven to 350°F. Coat 4 mini loaf pans with cooking spray.

2. Place oatmeal in a bowl; sift flour over top. Whisk egg with milk in another bowl; stir into oat mixture. Add cherries; stir to combine. Divide among prepared pans; smooth in an even layer.

3. Bake until a tester inserted in center of a loaf comes out clean, 20-25 minutes.

4. Let cool slightly in pan; remove and serve sprinkled with powdered sugar.

5. Serving size: 1 loaf

Bacon & Egg Breakfast Cups

Total Time: 0:30   **Prep:** 0:15   **Cook:** 0:15   **Serves:** 12   **Difficulty:** Easy

You'll love the convenience of this savory handheld breakfast. You can bake these cups ahead and keep them on hand for quick grab-and-go breakfasts; simply reheat in the microwave for 30 seconds to 1 minute. For easiest portability, bake the full 20 minutes to set the yolks fully; for looser yolks, you can bake for less time.

Ingredients

- Cooking spray — 4 spray(s) — 0
- Cooked Canadian bacon — 12 slice(s) — 5
- Egg(s) — 12 large egg(s) — 0
- Kosher salt — ¼ tsp — 0
- Black pepper — ¼ tsp — 0
- Grated Parmesan cheese — 2 Tbsp — 2
- Grape tomatoes — ¾ cup(s), chopped — 0
- Chives — 1 Tbsp, chopped — 0

Instructions

1. Preheat the oven to 400°F. Coat a 12-cup muffin pan with cooking spray.

2. Arrange 1 bacon slice in each muffin cup; if slices want to pop up, make a tear from the edge to the center and fit them down into the pan (they don't need to be perfect). Crack 1 egg into each muffin cup; sprinkle the eggs evenly with the salt and black pepper. Sprinkle the cheese evenly over the eggs, then sprinkle the tomatoes evenly over the top.

3. Bake until the eggs are set to your liking, 15 to 20 minutes. Sprinkle the chives evenly over the top.

4. Serving size: 1 egg cup

Easy Pancake Breakfast Tacos

Total Time: 0:10   **Prep:** 0:05   **Cook:** 0:05   **Serves:** 8   **Difficulty:** Easy

Here's a fun take on breakfast tacos, with pancakes standing in for tortillas. For ease and convenience, we call for frozen pancakes; their hearty texture is perfect here. To balance the slight sweetness of the pancakes, try using a spicy or smoky salsa.

Ingredients

Cooking spray — 0
4 spray(s)

Frozen pancake(s) — 22
8 item(s), about 36 grams each

Egg(s) — 0
6 large egg(s)

Kosher salt — 0
¼ tsp

Black pepper — 0
¼ tsp

Shredded reduced-fat Mexican-style cheese — 5
6 Tbsp

Fat free salsa — 0
8 tsp

Uncooked scallion(s) — 0
¼ cup(s), chopped

Instructions

1. Heat the pancakes according to the package directions; cover and keep warm.

2. In a medium bowl, whisk together the eggs, salt, and black pepper. Coat a medium nonstick skillet with cooking spray and heat over medium-low. Add the egg mixture to the pan; cook, stirring frequently to scramble, until the eggs are set, 3 to 4 minutes.

3. Arrange the pancakes on a work surface; top evenly with the scrambled eggs. Divide the cheese, salsa, and scallions evenly among the pancakes. Fold the pancakes over like a taco.

4. Serving size: 1 taco

Spinach, Feta & Tomato Breakfast Casserole

Total Time: 1:20 **Prep:** 0:15 **Cook:** 1:00 **Serves:** 8 **Difficulty:** Easy

This hearty breakfast gets a little Greek flair from oregano, spinach, and feta. It's an easy vegetarian option if you need to feed a crowd, but if you're serving a smaller group, the leftovers hold up and reheat well. Normally, you would use stale bread for this type of dish, but we start with soft sandwich bread and lightly toast it. We love fresh spinach here and find it easier to work with than frozen—you don't have to remember to thaw it, and you don't have to squeeze out all that water. If frozen is what you have on hand, though, it will work just fine.

Ingredients

Cooking spray — 0
4 spray(s)

Reduced-calorie oatmeal bread — 15
14 slice(s)

Fresh baby spinach — 0
10 oz

Low-fat milk — 9
2 ½ cup(s)

Dijon Mustard — 0
2 Tbsp

Dried oregano — 0
1 tsp

Garlic powder — 0
1 tsp

Kosher salt — 0
¾ tsp

Black pepper — 0
½ tsp

Egg(s) — 0
8 large egg(s)

Grape tomatoes — 0
1 cup(s), halved

Crumbled feta cheese — 14
¾ cup(s)

Instructions

1. Preheat the oven to 350°F. Stack a few pieces of bread and cut into cubes (about 9 per slice); repeat with the remaining bread. Spread the bread cubes onto a sheet pan. Bake at 350°F until lightly toasted, about 10 minutes, stirring after 5 minutes.

2. Meanwhile, coat a large nonstick skillet with cooking spray. Heat the pan over medium. Gradually add the spinach, tossing frequently with tongs until all of the spinach has been added and wilts, 3 to 4 minutes. Place the spinach in a colander or strainer set in the sink. Let stand for 5 minutes.

3. In a large bowl, whisk together the milk, mustard, oregano, garlic, salt, black pepper, and eggs. Stir in the spinach, untangling any clumps. Add the bread, tomatoes, and feta; toss gently to combine. Pour the mixture into a 13-by-9-inch baking dish coated with cooking spray. Bake at 350°F until the mixture is set and lightly browned and crusty on top, 50 to 55 minutes. Cut into 8 pieces and serve.

4. Serving size: 1 piece

Desayuno Tradicional (Breakfast Plate)

Total Time: 0:15   **Prep:** 0:10   **Cook:** 0:05   **Serves:** 1   **Difficulty:** Easy

For those who prefer savory breakfast to sweet, this classic Central American plate of hearty goodness is hard to beat. It combines scrambled eggs (you can cook them sunny-side up, if you prefer), a warm corn tortilla, smoky mashed black beans, and fresh vegetable accompaniments. The recipe makes one plate but is easy to scale up to serve more people.

Ingredients

Cooking spray — 0
2 spray(s)

Canned black beans — 0
½ cup(s), undrained

Smoked paprika — 0
¼ tsp

Corn tortilla(s) — 1
1 medium

Egg(s) — 0
2 large egg(s)

Table salt — 0
1 pinch(es)

Fresh tomato(es) — 0
2 slice(s)

Uncooked onion(s) — 0
1 thin slice(s)

Avocado — 2
¼ item(s), medium

Instructions

1. In a small microwave-safe bowl, mash the beans with a fork to your desired consistency; stir in the paprika. Cover and microwave on High until thoroughly heated, 45 seconds to 1 minute.

2. In a small nonstick skillet heated over medium-high or directly on a gas burner over medium-low, heat the tortilla until lightly charred, 30 seconds to 1 minute.

3. Off the heat, coat the skillet with cooking spray and heat over medium-low. In a small bowl, whisk together the eggs and salt. Add the egg mixture to the skillet; cook, stirring occasionally, until the eggs are scrambled, 2 to 3 minutes. Arrange the eggs, tortilla, beans, tomato, onion, and avocado on a plate.

Grilled Mexican Breakfast Tacos

Total Time: 0:25   Prep: 0:15   Cook: 0:10   Serves: 4   Difficulty: Easy

No need to relegate the grill to just lunches and dinners. When the weather is lovely, you'll enjoy firing it up and spending a little time outside cooking breakfast. While you cook the egg mixture in a cast-iron skillet on the grill, you can warm and char the tortillas on the grill rack around the pan.

Ingredients

Cooking spray — 0
4 spray(s)

Sweet mini baby bell pepper(s) — 0
4 item(s), sliced

Uncooked scallion(s) — 0
2 medium, thinly sliced

Corn tortilla(s) — 12
8 medium

Egg(s) — 0
8 large egg(s)

2% reduced fat milk — 1
3 Tbsp

Kosher salt — 0
¼ tsp

Salsa, restaurant type — 0
¾ cup(s)

Cilantro — 0
½ cup(s), leaves

Hot sauce — 0
4 tsp

Crumbled queso fresco cheese — 4
¼ cup(s)

Instructions

1 Coat a 10-inch cast-iron skillet with cooking spray. Set the pan on a grill; coat the grill rack around the pan with cooking spray. Close the grill lid, and heat the grill to medium-high (about 450°F).

2 When the grill and pan are hot, add the bell peppers and scallions to the skillet; sauté, stirring occasionally, for 3 minutes. As the vegetables cook, start warming the tortillas by arranging as many as will fit on the grill rack around the skillet; cook until lightly charred, about 20 seconds per side.

3 In a large bowl, whisk together the eggs, milk, and salt. Add the egg mixture to the vegetables in the skillet. Cook, stirring frequently to scramble, until the eggs are done, 4 to 5 minutes. Divide the egg mixture evenly among the tortillas; top the tacos evenly with salsa, cilantro, hot sauce, and cheese.

4 Serving size: 2 tacos

Easy Ham & Cheese Breakfast Quesadillas

Total Time: 0:25   Prep: 0:10   Cook: 0:15   Serves: 4   Difficulty: Easy

We love using a pizza stone on the grill to scramble the egg mixture and cook the quesadillas; the eggs pick up a faint smoky essence, and the assembled quesadillas get wonderfully crisp. You'll need to use a glazed pizza stone; a porous one won't work for cooking the eggs. If you don't have one, that's OK. You can scramble the eggs in a cast-iron skillet (heated on the grill) or on the stove, and then toast the quesadillas on a regular pizza stone.

Ingredients

Cooking spray — 0
4 spray(s)

Egg(s) — 0
6 large egg(s)

Kosher salt — 0
¼ tsp

Cooked Canadian bacon — 2
4 slice(s), chopped

Low carb, high fiber tortilla wrap(s) — 6
4 tortilla(s), about 1 1/2 oz each

Reduced-fat cheddar cheese — 10
¾ cup(s), shredded

Instructions

1. Place a pizza stone on a grill. Close the grill lid, and heat the grill to medium-high (about 450°F).

2. In a medium bowl, whisk together the eggs and salt. When the grill and pizza stone are hot, add the Canadian bacon to the pizza stone; cook, stirring occasionally, for 2 minutes. Spread the bacon in a ring toward the outer edge of the stone. Gradually add the egg mixture to the center of the stone, stirring constantly with a wooden or silicone spatula. (Go slowly so the egg doesn't run off the side of the stone.) Cook, stirring frequently, until the eggs are scrambled, about 3 minutes, folding in the bacon as they cook. Remove the egg mixture to a bowl; scrape off any remaining egg with a spatula.

3. Coat one side of each tortilla wrap with cooking spray. Turn the tortilla wraps over, coated side down. Sprinkle half of the cheese evenly over one side of the tortilla wraps; top evenly with the egg mixture and the remaining cheese. Fold the tortilla wraps in half and arrange on the hot pizza stone. Close the grill lid and cook until toasted and browned, 4 to 5 minutes per side.

4. Serving size: 1 quesadilla

Skillet breakfast sandwich hack

Total Time: 0:07 **Prep:** 0:05 **Cook:** 0:02 **Serves:** 1 **Difficulty:** Easy

Here's a fun way to make an egg sandwich all in one pan. The eggs go in first and then you place the bread right on top so the bread soaks in all the eggy deliciousness as they cook. The fillings are easy to customize: Go Greek with roasted peppers, dill, and feta, or try Italian with part-skim mozzarella, turkey pepperoni, and fresh basil. If you want some bacon with your sandwich, cook it in the pan first so your eggs can absorb all the bacon fat!

Ingredients

Egg(s) — 0
2 large egg(s), whisked

Table salt — 0
1 pinch(es)

Black pepper — 0
1 pinch(es)

Cooking spray — 0
2 spray(s)

Uncooked scallion(s) — 0
1 medium, thinly sliced

Reduced-fat cheddar cheese — 2
2 Tbsp

Light whole grain bread — 2
2 slice(s)

Fresh cherry tomato(es) — 0
4 medium, halved

Arugula — 0
½ cup(s), baby-variety

Instructions

1. In a small bowl, whisk eggs; stir in salt and pepper and set aside.

2. Coat a medium nonstick skillet with cooking spray; set over medium-high heat. When hot, add scallions to skillet; cook, stirring, 30 seconds. Pour eggs into skillet; sprinkle with cheese. Place bread over egg mixture (arranging slices so they are next to each other and the bottom edges are touching). Once eggs are cooked, using a large spatula, flip bread and eggs over all at the same time (so eggs are now on top).

3. Fold sides of cooked egg in so they are no longer hanging over bread; top with tomatoes and arugula. Flip one slice of bread over the other to form a sandwich; slice in half and serve immediately.

4. Serving size: 1 sandwich

Chapter 2:
Lunch

Tex-Mex Oatmeal Lunch Bowl

Total Time: 0:15   Prep: 0:10   Cook: 0:05   Serves: 1   Difficulty: Easy

Change up your midday grain bowl by using oatmeal as the base. You probably have it in your pantry already, it cooks up in a flash, and it pairs well with any topping you can think of. Here, we cook the oats in the microwave (at reduced power to keep them from boiling over) in vegetable broth for a savory boost, then top them with rotisserie chicken breast, pinto beans, corn, salsa, cheese, and avocado. It's like nachos, but in a creamy, more cozy form.

Ingredients

Fat free reduced sodium vegetable broth — 0
1 cup(s), or chicken broth

Uncooked old fashioned rolled oats — 3
½ cup(s)

Kosher salt — 0
1 pinch(es)

No-salt-added canned drained pinto beans — 0
¼ cup(s)

Frozen corn kernels — 0
¼ cup(s), thawed

Fat free salsa — 0
2 Tbsp

Skinless original seasoning rotisserie chicken breast — 0
2 oz, shredded

Cotija cheese — 0
1 ½ tsp, crumbled

Avocado — 2
¼ item(s), medium

Instructions

1. In a 4-cup glass measuring cup or a medium microwave-safe bowl, stir together the broth, oats, and salt. Microwave at 70% power until done, stirring once or twice, 4 to 5 minutes. Spoon the oats into a shallow bowl.

2. Meanwhile, heat a small nonstick skillet over medium heat. Add the beans, corn, salsa, and chicken; cook until heated through, stirring occasionally, 3 to 4 minutes. Spoon the mixture over the oats; top with the cheese and avocado.

3. Serving size: 1 bowl

Deconstructed Nachos Snack Lunch

Total Time: 0:15   **Prep:** 0:15   **Cook:** -   **Serves:** 2   **Difficulty:** Easy

Rotisserie chicken breast, black beans, corn, and pico de gallo come together quickly for a satisfying chunky mixture you can enjoy as a forkable salad or tortilla chip topper. Swap in black bean-and-corn salsa for the beans, corn, and pico, if you prefer. When packing this lunch, wrap the chips in a zip-top bag or loosely in plastic wrap to prevent them from sogging out.

Ingredients

Frozen corn kernels — 0
⅔ cup(s), thawed

Canned low sodium black beans — 0
⅔ cup(s), rinsed and drained

Pico de gallo — 0
⅔ cup(s)

Kosher salt — 0
¼ tsp

Ground cumin — 0
¼ tsp

Skinless original seasoning rotisserie chicken breast — 0
4 oz, chopped

Tortilla chips — 5
16 chip(s)

Fresh radish(es) — 0
8 medium, halved

Reduced fat pepper Jack cheese — 3
2 oz, sliced

Orange(s) — 0
1 medium, cut into 8 wedges

Instructions

1. In a medium bowl, stir together the corn, black beans, pico de gallo, salt, cumin, and chicken. Divide the chicken mixture evenly between 2 lunchboxes or portable containers. Arrange 8 tortilla chips, 8 radish halves, 1 ounce of cheese, and 4 orange wedges in each container.

2. Serving size: 1 lunchbox

Chickpea Salad Snack Lunch ③

Total Time: 0:15   **Prep:** 0:15   **Cook:** -   **Serves:** 2   **Difficulty:** Easy

With lots of fresh veggie accompaniments, this easy make-ahead lunch gives you plenty of opportunity to crunch your way through your midday meal. The centerpiece is a smashed chickpea salad—similar in feel to tuna or chicken salad but vegetarian.

Ingredients

Canned chickpeas — 0
1 ½ cup(s), rinsed and drained

Plain fat free Greek yogurt — 0
⅓ cup(s)

Uncooked scallion(s) — 0
¼ cup(s), chopped

Unsweetened dill pickle(s) — 0
2 Tbsp, finely chopped

Dijon Mustard — 0
2 tsp

Kosher salt — 0
⅛ tsp

Black pepper — 0
⅛ tsp

Cucumber(s) — 0
1 ⅓ cup(s), sliced

Olive(s) — 3
16 large

Uncooked celery — 0
2 rib(s), medium, medium, each cut into 3 pieces

Wafer rye crispbread crackers — 2
2 wafer(s)

Sweet red pepper(s) — 0
1 medium, cut into strips

Instructions

1 In a medium bowl, partially mash the chickpeas with a fork. Stir in the yogurt, scallions, pickles, mustard, salt, and pepper. Arrange about ¾ cup chickpea salad, ⅔ cup cucumber, 8 olives, 3 celery pieces, 1 cracker, and ½ sweet pepper in each of 2 lunchboxes or portable containers. Refrigerate for up to 4 days.

2 Serving size: 1 lunchbox

Snack Lunch Board

Total Time: 0:15   Prep: 0:15   Cook: -   Serves: 6   Difficulty: Easy

PSA: A lunch composed entirely of snack foods qualifies as a legit meal. Not only are these mix-and-match spreads simple to assemble but they also usually offer a little something for everyone in a picky crowd. Customizing as desired, aim for a combo of fresh fruit and veggies, a lean protein (like hummus), a crunchy carb (like pretzel thins), and maybe some chunks of cheese. No need to overthink it.

Ingredients

Store-bought hummus
¾ cup(s)

Unflavored pretzel thins
30 pretzel(s)

Small, thinly sliced turkey pepperoni
30 piece(s)

50% reduced fat sharp cheddar cheese
12 oz, cut into 24 cubes

Uncooked bell pepper(s)
1 cup(s), red or yellow, thinly sliced, or halved baby bell peppers

Uncooked baby carrots
15 item(s), or carrot sticks

Grapes
2 cup(s), seedless

Strawberries
1 cup(s), raw, halved

Fresh apple(s)
1 large, cored and cut into thin wedges

Instructions

1. Place the hummus in a small serving bowl. Set the bowl on a large platter. Fill the platter with piles of the remaining ingredients.

2. Serving size: 2 tbsp hummus, 5 pretzel thins, 5 pieces turkey pepperoni, 4 cubes cheddar, 1 cup fruit, and unlimited veggies

Bacon-Pepper Poppers Snack Lunch

Total Time: 0:30   **Prep:** 0:25   **Cook:** 0:05   **Serves:** 4   **Difficulty:** Easy

Some of the best on-the-go lunches are snack-based, ones that allow you to graze off and on as you find time. These well-curated bites include pepper poppers stuffed with bacon-and-herb cream cheese, plus a flexible cast of extras. Feel free to swap in any berries and veggies you like. Though we feature the peppers here as an anchor for make-ahead lunches, they're also fantastic appetizers for tailgating, block parties, or any casual gathering.

Ingredients

Low fat cream cheese — 8
3 oz

Plain fat free Greek yogurt — 0
¼ cup(s)

Uncooked celery — 0
2 Tbsp, finely chopped

Chives — 0
1 Tbsp, chopped, plus more for garnish

Dill — 0
2 tsp, chopped

Table salt — 0
¼ tsp

Black pepper — 0
¼ tsp

Cooked thick-sliced bacon — 6
3 slice(s), cooled and crumbled

Sweet mini baby bell pepper(s) — 0
8 item(s), halved and seeded

Strawberries — 0
32 medium

Olive(s) — 4
24 large

Uncooked baby carrots — 0
16 medium

Deli chicken breast — 0
8 oz, thinly sliced

Instructions

1. In medium bowl, combine cream cheese, yogurt, celery, 1 tbsp chives, dill, salt, and black pepper. Stir in bacon. Divide cream cheese among bell pepper halves. Garnish with more chives.

2. Arrange 4 stuffed pepper halves, 8 strawberries, 6 olives, 4 carrots, and 2 oz chicken in each of 4 lunch boxes or storage containers. Refrigerate for up to 4 days.

3. Serving size: 1 lunchbox

Lazy Deviled Egg Snack Lunch 4

Total Time: 0:18 **Prep:** 0:16 **Cook:** 0:02 **Serves:** 4 **Difficulty:** Easy

Perk up your desk lunch with a fun portable meal made up of irresistible snacks. It's a great way to fill up a bento-style lunchbox with colorful options that come together for a balanced meal. Better yet, it allows you to enjoy five (or more, if you like) different foods so that you don't get bored. The star of this meal is our lazy deviled eggs, made faster and easier by simply topping hard-boiled egg halves with Dijon mustard, dill pickles, and prosciuttto. Go ahead and meal-prep for the week; everything here will stay fresh and at peak flavor for three or four days.

Ingredients

Egg(s) — 0
4 large egg(s)

Dijon Mustard — 0
2 tsp

Kosher dill pickle sandwich slice(s) — 0
8 slice(s)

Prosciutto — 7
4 slice(s), about 1/2 oz each, halved lengthwise

Edamame in pods — 0
4 cup(s)

Smoked almonds — 8
40 piece(s)

Cantaloupe — 0
8 slice(s), each halved crosswise

Persian (mini) cucumber — 0
4 item(s), quartered lengthwise

Instructions

1 Place eggs in a medium saucepan and fill with enough water to cover eggs; bring to a boil for 2 minutes. Turn off heat and cover pan; let stand covered for 10 minutes. Place pan in sink and run cold water over eggs until cool. Peel eggs and slice each in half lengthwise. Top each egg half with ¼ tsp Dijon mustard and 1 pickle slice. Fold each prosciutto piece in half lengthwise and wrap around each egg half.

2 In each of 4 lunchboxes or portable containers, arrange 2 egg halves, 1 cup edamame, 10 almonds, 4 cantaloupe pieces, and 4 cucumber quarters. Refrigerate up to 4 days.

3 Serving size: 1 lunchbox

Cranberry-Sage Chicken Meatballs

6

Total Time: 0:45 **Prep:** 0:20 **Cook:** 0:25 **Serves:** 4 **Difficulty:** Easy

These chicken meatballs come together in a snap, are baked in the oven for ease and convenience, and have a surprise ingredient that's not only packed with nutrition but helps keep the meatballs moist and flavorful: canned pumpkin puree! Enjoy the meatballs with your favorite grain, over greens, or as part of a grain bowl. Dress them up with a sprinkle of feta or ricotta salata, and some fresh herbs, if desired. The meatballs freeze well so consider making a double batch for an easy dinner another time.

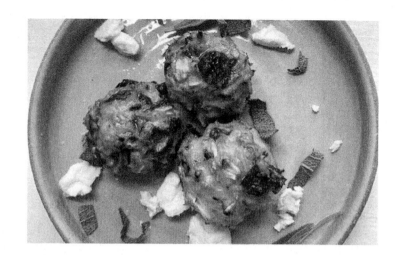

Ingredients

Cooking spray — 0
4 spray(s)

Canned pumpkin puree — 0
¾ cup(s)

Fresh mushroom(s) — 0
¾ cup(s), finely chopped

Uncooked rolled oats — 3
½ cup(s)

Uncooked onion(s) — 0
½ small, finely chopped

Reduced sugar dried cranberries — 4
¼ cup(s), finely chopped

Garlic clove — 0
1 clove(s), large, minced

Kosher salt — 0
1 ¼ tsp

Ground cumin — 0
1 tsp

Uncooked 93% lean ground chicken — 18
1 pound(s)

Fresh sage — 0
1 tsp, minced

Lemon(s) — 0
½ item(s)

Instructions

1. Preheat oven to 425°F. Line a baking sheet with parchment and lightly coat it with cooking spray.

2. In a large bowl, thoroughly combine the pumpkin, mushrooms, oats, onion, cranberries, garlic, salt, and cumin. Add the chicken and sage, and gently combine. Shape into 20 meatballs (about 2 tbsp each) and transfer to the prepared baking sheet.

3. Bake, turning after 15 minutes, until cooked through, about 25 to 30 minutes (meatballs should reach an internal temperature of 165°F). Let rest for 5 minutes. Transfer to a serving bowl and drizzle with lemon juice.

4. Serving size: 5 meatballs

Air-fried Crounon-crusted salmon by Carrington Farms

Total Time: 0:30   **Prep:** 0:10   **Cook:** 0:10   **Serves:** 4   **Difficulty:** Easy

To easily crush the Crounons, place them in a zip-close plastic bag, and use a mallet or rolling pin to gently crush them to a bread crumb consistency.

Ingredients

Uncooked skinless wild salmon fillet
1 pound(s), four 4 oz pieces

Extra virgin olive oil
1 Tbsp

Fresh lemon juice
1 Tbsp

Table salt
4 pinch(es)

Black pepper
4 pinch(es)

Carrington Farms Organic Crounons, garlic & parmesan
¼ cup(s), crushed

Instructions

1. Rinse salmon with water; pat dry. Rub salmon with oil; season with salt and pepper. Drizzle with lemon; let sit while air-fryer heats.

2. Preheat air-fryer to 390°F.

3. Pour crushed Crounons onto a plate. Press tops of salmon fillets into crumbs until they are well-coated.

4. Place fillets, crumb side up, in air-fryer basket; coat with cooking spray (optional). Air-fry until breading is crisp and fish is cooked through, about 10 to 12 minutes.

5. Serving size: 1 salmon fillet

Turkey tortilla wedges with arugula and pine nuts

9

Total Time: 0:18   Prep: 0:10   Cook: 0:08   Serves: 4   Difficulty: Easy

This quick lunch or dinner is part tortilla pizza and part tostada, with Eastern Mediterranean and Middle Eastern flavors in the mix. One of those standout flavors is Sumac, which is made from the dried and ground berries of the sumac bush. It lends a tart, slightly acidic flavor to this dish, and is a common spice in Middle Eastern cooking. Here it works its magic on ground turkey, along with shallots, garlic, tomatoes, cilantro, and feta to make a delicious topping for these crispy tortillas. Once the filling is perfect, it gets piled on the tortillas, and then topped with arugula and pine nuts, and served with fresh lemon. So good, so simple, and so quick!

Ingredients

8" flour tortilla(s) — 19
4 item(s)

Olive oil — 6
4 tsp

Uncooked boneless skinless turkey breast — 0
¾ pound(s), ground

Table salt — 0
¼ tsp

Uncooked shallot(s) — 0
1 large, halved and thinly sliced

Garlic — 0
2 large clove(s), minced

Fresh cherry tomato(es) — 0
1 cup(s), quartered

Ground sumac — 0
2 tsp

Canned tomato paste — 0
1 tsp

Water — 0
⅓ cup(s)

Crumbled feta cheese — 6
⅓ cup(s)

Cilantro — 0
3 Tbsp, fresh, chopped

Arugula — 0
½ cup(s), baby

Pine nuts — 3
2 Tbsp, toasted

Lemon(s) — 0
½ item(s), cut into wedges

Instructions

1. Preheat oven to 400°F.

2. Place tortillas on large baking sheet in single layer and brush tops with 1 teaspoon oil. Bake until crisp, about 8 minutes.

3. Meanwhile, heat 2 teaspoons oil in large skillet over medium-high heat. Add turkey and salt; cook, stirring occasionally, until turkey is no longer pink, about 2 minutes. Add remaining 1 teaspoon oil to skillet. Add shallot and garlic and cook, stirring often, until shallot is softened, about 2 minutes. Add tomatoes, sumac, and tomato paste and cook, stirring constantly, 1 minute. Stir in water and cook, stirring with wooden spoon to scrape up browned bits from bottom of pan, about 1 minute. Remove from heat; stir in feta and cilantro.

4. Top tortillas evenly with turkey mixture, then top evenly with arugula and pine nuts. Cut each tortilla into 4 wedges. Serve with lemon wedges.

5. Serving size: 4 wedges

Instant Classic Chicken Noodle Soup for One

Total Time: 0:10   Prep: 0:07   Cook: 0:03   Serves: 1   Difficulty: Easy

This six-ingredient, 10-minute soup is perfect for those days when a craving hits (or you're under the weather) but you don't want tons of leftovers. It's also an ideal portable lunch option, particularly if you have leftover chicken sitting in your fridge. Fresh pasta, couscous, and Asian noodles that only require a soak (like rice sticks) all work well in mason jar noodle soups. Another option: leftover cooked dried pasta and noodles. Fresh dill really is worth it here for the bright flavor it adds as well as its pretty delicate leaves. But, you can substitute 1/4 teaspoon of dried dill, if you have that on hand.

Ingredients

Reduced-sodium chicken stock base — 1
2 tsp

Uncooked onion(s) — 0
1 Tbsp, chopped, finely chopped

Frozen peas and carrots — 0
¼ cup(s)(no need to thaw)

Cooked skinless boneless chicken breast(s) — 0
2 oz, chopped

Cooked egg noodles — 3
½ cup(s)

Dill — 0
1 tsp, fresh, chopped

Instructions

1. In a pint-sized mason jar or container with a tight-fitting lid, layer ingredients in order listed. Close jar; refrigerate until ready to use.

2. Fill jar with boiling water (about 2 cups). Stir very well, until soup base is fully dissolved. Close jar; let sit for 3 minutes.

3. Remove lid; stir once.

4. Serving size: 1 jar

Cheeseburger Bowls

Total Time: 0:25   Prep: 0:15   Cook: 0:10   Serves: 4   Difficulty: Easy

So you want a cheeseburger with all the fixings, but you're fixing to be healthy? This colorful meal has your name written all over it.

Ingredients

- Cooking spray — 0
  4 spray(s)
- Uncooked extra lean ground beef 96% lean 4% fat — 12
  1 pound(s)
- Kosher salt — 0
  1 tsp
- Uncooked onion(s) — 0
  1 small, finely chopped
- Chopped romaine lettuce — 0
  6 cup(s), shredded
- Plum tomato(es) — 0
  4 medium, diced
- Kosher dill pickle sandwich slice(s) — 0
  15 slice(s), divided
- Reduced-fat cheddar cheese — 7
  8 Tbsp, shredded
- Uncooked red onion(s) — 0
  6 thin slice(s), optional
- Ketchup — 1
  1 Tbsp
- Light mayonnaise — 3
  2 Tbsp
- Mustard — 0
  1½ tsp
- Worcestershire sauce — 0
  ½ tsp

Instructions

1. Coat a large nonstick skillet with cooking spray and heat over medium-high. Add the beef and salt. Reserve 1 tbsp of the yellow onion and add the remaining yellow onion to the skillet. Cook, breaking up the meat with a wooden spoon, until the beef is cooked through and no longer pink, 7 to 9 minutes. Let cool. Set aside.

2. Meanwhile, place 1½ cups lettuce each in 4 medium bowls. Top each bowl with a quarter of the tomato, 3 pickle slices, 2 tbsp cheese, and the red onion (if using).

3. In a small bowl, stir the ketchup, mayonnaise, mustard, Worcestershire sauce, and reserved 1 tbsp yellow onion. Finely chop the remaining 3 dill pickle slices and add to the bowl.

4. Divide the beef mixture among the bowls of lettuce. Serve with the special sauce.

5. Serving size: 1 bowl (about 2 cups)

Shortcut-Shrimp Fried Rice

Total Time: 0:15 **Prep:** 0:07 **Cook:** 0:08 **Serves:** 1 **Difficulty:** Easy

Convenience foods like frozen cooked shrimp and frozen cooked rice, shredded carrots, and a big batch of roasted veggies in the fridge, are key to getting this meal on the table fast. You don't even need to defrost the rice or shrimp first since they thaw and cook quickly in a pan over medium-high heat.

Ingredients

Cooking spray — 0
4 spray(s)

Non starchy roasted vegetables without oil — 0
1 cup(s), such as broccoli

Cooked medium grain brown rice — 6
1 cup(s)

Cooked frozen shrimp — 0
3 oz

Egg(s) — 0
1 large egg(s)

Shredded carrot(s) — 0
½ cup(s)

Low sodium soy sauce — 0
1 Tbsp, or to taste

Uncooked scallion(s) — 0
2 Tbsp, sliced

Instructions

1 Heat a nonstick skillet coated with cooking spray over medium-high heat; add roasted vegetables, rice, and shrimp; toss and heat through.

2 Push rice mixture to side of pan and crack egg in middle; scramble egg. Stir egg into rice mixture, add carrots and sprinkle with soy sauce; warm through and garnish with scallions.

3 Makes 1 serving.

Easy Buffalo Chicken Salad

Total Time: 0:05   Prep: 0:05   Cook: -   Serves: 1   Difficulty: Easy

Classic Buffalo chicken gets the salad treatment in this easy, no-cook recipe. Feel free to dial the heat up or down and experiment with different crunchy veggies to add to the mix, like fresh bell pepper strips, shredded cabbage, corn kernels, or cucumbers.

Ingredients

Cooked skinless boneless chicken breast(s)
2 oz, shredded

Reduced fat crumbled blue cheese
¼ cup(s)

Light mayonnaise
1 Tbsp

Hot sauce
1 Tbsp

Table salt
2 pinch(es)

Black pepper
1 pinch(es)

Fresh radish(es)
¼ cup(s), sliced

Uncooked carrot(s)
¼ cup(s), shredded

Uncooked celery
1 rib(s), medium, thinly sliced

Mixed greens
2 cup(s)

Instructions

1. In a medium bowl, toss the chicken, blue cheese, mayonnaise, hot sauce, salt, and pepper until well combined. Add the radishes, carrots, and celery. Toss to combine.

2. Arrange the greens in a shallow bowl. Top with the chicken mixture.

Crounon-crusted chicken Parmesan by Carrington Farms

Total Time: 1:20 **Prep:** 0:20 **Cook:** 1:00 **Serves:** 4 **Difficulty:** Easy

Seasoned, gluten-free, quinoa croutons are crushed and used as the breading for this crispy baked chicken parm recipe. It's delicious served over pasta or zoodles, or served over your favorite toasted bread.

Ingredients

Coconut oil spray — 0
4 second spray(s)

Water — 0
¼ cup(s)

Egg(s) — 0
1 large egg(s), beaten

Carrington Farms Organic Crounons, garlic & parmesan — 7
½ cup(s), crushed

Grated Parmesan cheese — 2
2 Tbsp, divided

Italian seasoning — 0
2 tsp

Uncooked boneless skinless chicken breast — 0
1 pound(s), four 4 oz pieces

Store-bought marinara sauce — 4
1 cup(s)

Shredded part-skim mozzarella cheese — 6
½ cup(s)

Instructions

1. Preheat oven to 350°F. Coat a 9- X 13-inch baking dish with cooking spray.

2. In a shallow bowl, whisk together water and egg. In another shallow bowl, combine crushed Crounons, 1 tbsp Parmesan, and Italian seasoning.

3. Dip a piece of chicken in egg mixture; turn to coat. Next, dip chicken in Crounon mixture; turn to coat. Then dip the same piece of chicken in egg mixture and Crounon mixture once more to create a double coating. Place chicken on prepared pan; repeat with remaining ingredients.

4. Bake for 40 minutes. Remove from oven; divide marinara sauce and cheese over chicken. Return to oven and bake until chicken reaches an internal temperature of 165°F, about 15 to 20 minutes more. (Broil for 2 to 3 minutes for extra browning, if desired.)

5. Serving size: 1 chicken cutlet

Shrimp, pepper & snap pea sauté

Total Time: 0:33 **Prep:** 0:25 **Cook:** 0:08 **Serves:** 4 **Difficulty:** Easy

This simple dish makes a bowl full of crunchy vegetables, tender sweet shrimp and a richly flavored glossy Asian inspired sauce in just 30 minutes. Great for an easy weeknight meal, the combination of snap peas, bell peppers and shrimp are so colorful with the sauce and seasonings, you may want to make this for a larger crowd. The jalapeno adds some spice to the stir-fried vegetables and chili-garlic sauce adds another layer and more kinds of flavor. Choose your level of spice by adding more or less of those to the dish. Serve this gorgeous saute over quickly cooked cauliflower rice or hot cooked rice stick noodles.

Ingredients

Fat free chicken broth — ¾ cup(s)

Low sodium soy sauce — 2 Tbsp, divided

Cornstarch — 1 ½ tsp

Dry sherry — 1 tsp

Uncooked shrimp — 1 pound(s), large, peeled, deveined

Cooking spray — 4 spray(s)

Sweet red pepper(s) — 1 large, cut into thin strips

Yellow pepper(s) — 1 large, cut into thin strips

Uncooked sugar snap peas — 1 cup(s), strings removed

Jalapeño pepper(s) — 1 small, seeded and minced

Uncooked scallion(s) — 4 medium, minced (plus extra for garnish)

Minced garlic — 1 ½ Tbsp

Minced ginger — 1 ½ Tbsp

Cilantro — ½ cup(s), chopped

Sesame oil — ¼ tsp

Garlic chili paste — ⅛ tsp, or to taste

Instructions

1 Combine broth and 1 Tbsp soy sauce in a small bowl.

2 In a medium bowl, combine cornstarch, remaining 1 Tbsp soy sauce and sherry. Add shrimp and toss to coat; set aside.

3 Coat a large nonstick skillet with cooking spray; heat over medium-high heat. Add peppers, snap peas and jalapeño; stir-fry for 1 minute. Add scallions, garlic and ginger; cook until fragrant, 30 seconds.

4 Add shrimp and any liquid in bowl to skillet; stir-fry until shrimp are pink and opaque, 2-3 minutes.

5 Add broth mixture; cook, stirring a few times, until sauce thickens a little, 1 minute. Stir in cilantro and oil; garnish with optional chili garlic paste and chopped scallions.

6 Serving size: 1 cup

Ponzu Chicken

Total Time: 1:40 **Prep:** 0:20 **Cook:** 0:20 **Serves:** 4 **Difficulty:** Easy

You'll love this chicken dish so much, you can make extra to have on hand throughout the week since it can be used in a variety of dishes. The chicken and (boiled) marinade can be refrigerated, together or in separate containers, for up to 3 days. Both are good cold or reheated. If you're serving right away, the chicken is delicious just out of the skillet, drizzled with the sauce and served over wilted spinach or with rice, quinoa, or another grain. Or turn it into a lettuce wrap like we did here, cutting the chicken into bite-size pieces; adding a few crunchy ingredients, such as grated jicama, shredded carrots, sprouts, cucumber and/or peanuts; and sprinkling everything with the marinade.

Ingredients

Fresh lemon(s) with peel — 1
1 item(s), or lime, zested and juiced

Ponzu sauce — 1
¼ cup(s)

Rice vinegar — 0
2 Tbsp

Olive oil — 3
2 tsp, or vegetable oil

Thai curry paste — 1
1 tsp, red variety (or sambal oelek or chile paste with garlic)

Sugar — 1
½ tsp

Sea salt — 0
1 pinch(es), fine variety

Uncooked boneless skinless chicken breast — 0
1 ¼ pound(s), four 5 oz pieces

Olive oil — 4
1 Tbsp, or vegetable oil

Instructions

1. Mix everything together, except chicken and 1 Tbsp oil, in a zip-close plastic bag or large bowl. Taste and see if you'd like more of any ingredient — you might want a bit more heat.

2. Add chicken to marinade, turn over to coat, and seal bag or cover bowl. Marinate 1 hour at room temperature or up to 1 day in refrigerator.

3. If you've chilled the chicken, take it out of refrigerator about 30 minutes before you're ready to cook. Remove chicken from marinade (reserve marinade); pat chicken dry.

4. Pour remaining 1 Tbsp oil into a large nonstick skillet set over medium heat. When oil is hot, add chicken. Cook, uncovered, 4 minutes on each side; then cook, covered, 4-5 minutes more. Test for doneness by inserting an instant-read thermometer in thickest part of chicken (should be 165°F); transfer chicken to a serving dish.

5. Discard whatever oil is in pan and carefully wipe pan clean with paper towels. Pour in reserved marinade and bring to a boil. Boil 2 minutes, then pour sauce over chicken.

6. Serving size: 1 chicken breast and about 2 Tbsp sauce

Asian Mango-Cucumber Salad with Grilled Shrimp

Total Time: 0:31 **Prep:** 0:25 **Cook:** 0:06 **Serves:** 4 **Difficulty:** Easy

Sweet meets heat in this lovely mango-cucumber salad. It's substantial enough for dinner and takes only about a half an hour to make. The dressing comes together in minutes and features fresh lime zest and juice, rice vinegar, fish sauce, brown sugar, and Sriracha for a touch of heat. If you're spice-averse, feel free to leave it out, but we love the contrast in flavor with the sweet brown sugar and funky fish sauce. It also nicely complements the cucumbers, mangoes, and onion. Also, we left the tails on for the shrimp for a pretty presentation, but you can definitely cut them off if your prefer.

Ingredients

- **Cooking spray** — 2 spray(s) — 0
- **Lime zest** — ½ tsp — 0
- **Fresh lime juice** — 2 Tbsp — 0
- **Rice vinegar** — ½ Tbsp — 0
- **Fish sauce** — 1 tsp — 0
- **Dark brown sugar** — 1 tsp — 1
- **Sriracha hot sauce** — ½ tsp — 0
- **Uncooked red onion(s)** — 1 small — 0
- **Cucumber(s)** — 1 medium, cut crosswise in half — 0
- **Mango(es)** — 1 large, ripe but firm, peeled, pitted, cut in matchsticks — 0
- **Fresh mint leaves** — ⅓ cup(s), packed, thinly sliced — 0
- **Basil** — ⅓ cup(s), packed, thinly sliced — 0
- **Dark sesame oil** — 1 tsp — 1
- **Table salt** — ½ tsp — 0
- **Black pepper** — ¼ tsp, freshly ground — 0
- **Uncooked shrimp** — 1 pound(s), extra-large, peeled, deveined — 0

Instructions

1. Off heat, coat a grill or grill pan with cooking spray. Preheat to medium heat.

2. Meanwhile, in a small bowl, whisk together lime zest and juice, vinegar, fish sauce, sugar and Sriracha.

3. Cut onion crosswise in half; spiralize 1 piece with slicer blade (save remaining onion half for another use). Place onion in a strainer and rinse under cold running water; pat dry. Tear onion into 4-inch pieces; add to a large bowl.

4. Spiralize cucumber halves with slicer blade; tear into 4-inch pieces. Add to large bowl with mango, mint and basil. Drizzle with dressing; toss gently to coat.

5. Combine sesame oil, salt and pepper in a medium bowl; add shrimp and toss to coat. Grill shrimp until cooked through (opaque) and slightly firm, about 3 minutes per side; serve over salad.

Chicken piccata stir-fry

Total Time: 0:25   Prep: 0:20   Cook: 0:05   Serves: 4   Difficulty: Easy

In this quick stove-top dish, classic Italian chicken piccata meets Asian stir-fry when prepared in a wok along with the addition of soy sauce, string beans and peanut oil. A light coating of cornstarch gives this chicken a nice brown color and a crispy exterior and it also aids in thickening the sauce. Lemon brightens the flavor of this stir-fry and should be added once the food is plated. If an acidic ingredient like lemon juice is added to the wok, it will ruin the pan's patina. For variation, small broccoli florets would make a good swap for the beans.

Ingredients

Uncooked boneless skinless chicken breast — 0
1 pound(s), cut into ¼-inch-thick slices

Dry sherry — 2
3 Tbsp, divided

Cornstarch — 1
2 tsp, divided

Table salt — 0
¾ tsp, divided

Black pepper — 0
¼ tsp, freshly ground

Fat free chicken broth — 0
½ cup(s)

Low sodium soy sauce — 0
1 Tbsp

Peanut oil — 6
4 tsp, or vegetable oil

Uncooked shallot(s) — 0
1 medium, thinly sliced

Minced garlic — 0
1 Tbsp

Uncooked string beans — 0
2 cup(s), cut into 2-inch pieces

Capers — 0
1 Tbsp, rinsed

Fresh parsley — 0
2 Tbsp, chopped

Lemon(s) — 0
½ medium, cut into 4 wedges

Instructions

1 In medium bowl, combine chicken, 1 tbsp sherry, 1 tsp cornstarch, ½ tsp salt, and black pepper. In small bowl, combine broth, soy sauce, and remaining 2 tbsp sherry and 1 tsp cornstarch.

2 Heat 14-inch flat-bottomed wok or 12-inch skillet over high until drop of water evaporates within 1 to 2 seconds of contact. Swirl 1 tbsp oil in wok. Add shallot and garlic and stir-fry until fragrant, about 10 seconds. Push shallot and garlic to sides of wok and add chicken, spreading evenly into 1 layer in wok. Cook, undisturbed, for 1 minute so chicken begins to sear. Stir-fry until chicken is no longer pink but not cooked through, about 1 minute.

3 Swirl remaining 1 tsp oil in wok. Add green beans and capers and sprinkle with remaining ¼ tsp salt and stir-fry just until combined, about 30 seconds. Swirl in broth mixture and stir-fry until chicken is cooked through and sauce is slightly thickened, 1 to 2 minutes. Sprinkle with parsley. Serve with lemon wedges.

4 Serving size: 1 cup

Chicken sausage, mushroom and pasta casserole

9

Total Time: 1:10 **Prep:** 0:20 **Cook:** 0:50 **Serves:** 8 **Difficulty:** Easy

Pasta meets pizza in this comforting one-dish meal. It can be prepared a day or two ahead – perfect for busy weeknights. Assemble the casserole as directed but set aside the mozzarella cheese, 1/2 cup of the sauce and the breadcrumbs. Wrap the casserole tightly with plastic wrap and refrigerate up to 2 days. When ready to bake, let the casserole come to room temperature and then drizzle with the reserved sauce. Sprinkle with the cheese and breadcrumbs and bake as directed above. Place your casserole under the broiler for a minute after it's finished cooking, if you prefer your casseroles well-browned.

Ingredients

Cooking spray — 0
2 spray(s)

Uncooked whole wheat pasta — 26
12 oz, rotini suggested (about 3 cups)

Olive oil — 1
1 tsp, extra-virgin

Panko breadcrumbs — 6
½ cup(s)

Grated Parmesan cheese — 2
2 Tbsp, Parmigiano-Reggiano suggested

Dried oregano — 0
1 tsp

Cooked chicken sausage(s) — 8
8 oz, Italian-variety, thinly sliced

Yellow pepper(s) — 0
1 medium, thinly sliced

Uncooked onion(s) — 0
1 medium, chopped

Fresh mushroom(s) — 0
1 pound(s), sliced

Water — 0
2 Tbsp

Marinara sauce — 14
4 cup(s)

Shredded part-skim mozzarella cheese — 11
1 cup(s)

Instructions

1. Preheat oven to 350°F. Coat a 9- X 13-inch baking dish with cooking spray.

2. Cook pasta according to package directions; drain pasta and return to pot.

3. Meanwhile, heat oil in a large nonstick skillet over medium heat. Add breadcrumbs and reduce heat to medium-low; cook, stirring often, until toasted, about 4 minutes. Remove breadcrumbs to a small bowl; stir in Parmesan and oregano and set aside.

4. In same skillet, cook sausage over medium-high heat, stirring frequently, until browned, about 5 minutes; remove to a plate and drain any fat from skillet.

5. Add pepper and onion to skillet; cook over medium-high heat, stirring frequently, until vegetables start to brown and soften, about 5 minutes.

6. Add mushrooms and water to skillet; cook, stirring frequently, until vegetables are tender, about 8 minutes.

7. Add vegetables, sausage and marinara sauce to pot with drained pasta; toss to coat. Spoon into prepared baking dish and sprinkle with mozzarella and reserved breadcrumbs. Bake until heated through and cheese melts, about 25 minutes. Slice into 8 pieces and serve. Yields 1 piece per serving (about 1 1/2 cups).

Chapter 3:
Dinner

Chicken Sancocho

Total Time: 1:10   **Prep:** 0:20   **Cook:** 0:50   **Serves:** 6   **Difficulty:** Easy

This poultry version of the Latin American classic is chock full of hearty ingredients, including potatoes, yuca (also known as cassava), and plantains. Rich, meaty, bone-in chicken thighs simmer in the broth so they impart more flavor; after they're done, the meat gets shredded and stirred into the soup. Everyone gets to enjoy a large, deeply satisfying serving.

Ingredients

Olive oil — 4
1 Tbsp

Uncooked onion(s) — 0
1 medium, chopped

Garlic — 0
6 large clove(s), minced

Fresh tomato(es) — 0
1 cup(s), chopped

Ground cumin — 0
1 tsp

No-salt-added chicken stock — 2
6 cup(s)

Kosher salt — 0
1 ½ tsp

Uncooked yuca — 15
1 ½ cup(s), fresh or frozen, peeled and cut into bite-sized pieces

Uncooked red potato(es) — 6
¾ pound(s), baby variety, halved (or quartered if large)

Uncooked plantain(s) — 8
1 medium, green, peeled and cut into bite-sized pieces

Uncooked bone in skinless chicken thigh(s) — 19
1 ¾ pound(s)

Cilantro — 0
¾ cup(s)

Fresh yellow corn — 0
3 medium, each cut into 4 pieces

Instructions

1. Heat the oil in a Dutch oven over medium. Add the onion and garlic; cook until softened, about 5 minutes, stirring occasionally. Add the tomatoes and cumin; cook 1 minute, stirring frequently. Stir in the chicken stock, salt, yuca, potatoes, and plantain; bring to a boil over high heat. Add the chicken; cover, reduce the heat to low, and simmer until the chicken is done and the vegetables are tender, about 30 minutes.

2. Remove the chicken from the pot; cool slightly. Add ½ cup cilantro and corn to the pot; cook until the corn is crisp-tender, 7 to 8 minutes. Pull the chicken meat from the bones; discard the bones. Shred the chicken and stir into the soup. Sprinkle with the remaining ¼ cup cilantro.

3. Serving size: about 2 cups

Grilled chicken sandwich with smoky honey mustard

Total Time: 0:35 **Prep:** 0:10 **Cook:** 0:10 **Serves:** 4 **Difficulty:** Easy

Our easy herb-marinated chicken sandwich, with its finishing touch of sweet-smoky honey mustard, is more delicious than its fast-food counterpart, with fresher veggie toppings and super-moist, just-off-the grill chicken. You can use either an outdoor grill or a stovetop grill pan; if using the latter, be sure to follow our instructions to loosely tent the pan with foil so that you create an environment similar to a closed grill.

Ingredients

Cooking spray — 0
4 spray(s)

Uncooked boneless skinless chicken breast(s) — 0
1 pound(s), 4 (4-oz) cutlets

Light Italian dressing — 2
4 Tbsp

Dijon Mustard — 0
2 ½ Tbsp

Light mayonnaise — 2
1 ½ Tbsp

Honey — 5
1 Tbsp

Smoked paprika — 0
½ tsp

Light whole wheat hamburger buns — 8
4 bun(s)

Lettuce — 0
4 leaf/leaves, large

Fresh tomato(es) — 0
4 slice(s)

Instructions

1. Arrange the chicken in a single layer in an 11 x 7–inch baking dish. Pierce the chicken all over with a fork. Drizzle the dressing over the chicken, and turn the chicken to coat. Marinate at room temperature for 15 minutes, turning the chicken over occasionally.

2. Coat an outdoor grill rack or a large stovetop grill pan with cooking spray. Preheat the grill or grill pan to medium-high. Remove the chicken from the marinade, allowing any excess marinade to fall back into the dish; discard the excess marinade. Arrange the chicken on the grill rack or grill pan. Close the grill lid, or tent the grill pan loosely with foil. Grill until the chicken is well marked and cooked through, 4 to 5 minutes per side.

3. Meanwhile, in a small bowl, whisk together the mustard, mayonnaise, honey, and smoked paprika. Spread the sauce evenly over both sides of the buns. On the bottom half of each bun, arrange 1 chicken cutlet, 1 lettuce leaf, 1 tomato slice, and top half of the bun.

4. Serving size: 1 sandwich

Oven-roasted chicken breast with a simple salad ③

Total Time: 0:35 **Prep:** 0:15 **Cook:** 0:20 **Serves:** 2 **Difficulty:** Easy

Double or triple the chicken part of this recipe for meals later in the week: Chop the chicken and use it in grain bowls, make chicken salad sandwiches, or add some to pasta dishes. Save time by swapping in your favorite creamy light Italian dressing.

Ingredients

- Cooking spray — 4 spray(s) — **0**
- Fresh thyme — 1 sprig(s), leaves — **0**
- Rosemary — 1 sprig(s), leaves — **0**
- Olive oil — 1 Tbsp — **4**
- Table salt — 2 pinch(es), divided (to taste) — **0**
- Black pepper — 2 pinch(es), divided (to taste) — **0**
- Uncooked boneless skinless chicken breast(s) — 8 oz, 2 [4 oz] pieces — **0**
- Cooking spray — 4 spray(s) — **0**
- Fresh thyme — 1 sprig(s), leaves — **0**
- Rosemary — 1 sprig(s), leaves — **0**
- Olive oil — 1 Tbsp — **4**
- Table salt — 2 pinch(es), divided (to taste) — **0**
- Black pepper — 2 pinch(es), divided (to taste) — **0**
- Uncooked boneless skinless chicken breast(s) — 8 oz, 2 [4 oz] pieces — **0**

Instructions

1. Preheat oven to 400ºF. Coat a small, shallow roasting pan with cooking spray.

2. In a small bowl, combine the herbs, oil, and pinch each salt and pepper. Place the chicken on the prepared pan and drizzle the oil mixture over top.

3. Bake until the chicken is cooked through, about 20 to 25 minutes.

4. Meanwhile, in a small bowl, combine the yogurt with the lemon zest and lemon juice. Season to taste with salt and pepper. Place the lettuce, tomatoes, and yellow pepper in a medium bowl and toss with the dressing.

5. Serving size: 1 piece of chicken and about 1 1/2 cups salad

Chicken Caesar salad wrap (6)

Total Time: 0:10   Prep: 0:10   Cook: -   Serves: 1   Difficulty: Easy

A twist on a typical chicken salad, this simple, no-cook recipe gets its jolt of flavor from zingy Caesar dressing and tangy yogurt standing in for the usual mayonnaise. Almonds add an unexpected crunch and more protein (plus good-for-you fats) while crisp romaine keeps things fresh.

Ingredients

- Cooked skinless boneless chicken breast(s) — ½ cup(s), chopped (0)
- Light Caesar dressing — 1 Tbsp (1)
- Plain fat free Greek yogurt — 1 Tbsp (0)
- Dijon Mustard — 1 Tbsp (0)
- Fresh lemon juice — 2 tsp (0)
- Garlic powder — ½ tsp (0)
- Table salt — 2 pinch(es) (0)
- Black pepper — 1 pinch(es) (0)
- Sliced almonds — 2 Tbsp, toasted (2)
- 8" whole wheat sandwich wrap(s) — 1 wrap(s) (3)
- Romaine lettuce — 1 cup(s), shredded, torn (0)

Instructions

1. In a medium bowl, stir together the chicken, Caesar dressing, yogurt, mustard, lemon juice, garlic powder, salt, and pepper. Fold in the almonds.

2. Arrange the chicken salad down the middle of the wrap. Top with the lettuce. Fold in sides of the wrap and roll up to close.

3. Serving size: 1 wrap

Sheet pan chicken gyros

Total Time: 0:55 **Prep:** 0:20 **Cook:** 0:25 **Serves:** 4 **Difficulty:** Easy

A thick, garlicky, well spiced yogurt marinade deliciously coats bite-sized pieces of chicken. The chicken cooks alongside a colorful mix of bell peppers and onions, then the whole pan goes under the broiler to pick up a little bit of tasty char. All gets tucked into pitas and finished with creamy tzatziki.

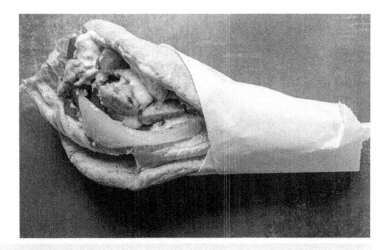

Ingredients

- **Plain fat free Greek yogurt** — ¼ cup(s) — 0
- **Fresh lemon juice** — 2 Tbsp — 0
- **Olive oil** — 2 Tbsp, divided — 9
- **Ground cumin** — 1 tsp — 0
- **Dried oregano** — ¾ tsp — 0
- **Kosher salt** — ¾ tsp, divided — 0
- **Black pepper** — ¾ tsp, divided — 0
- **Smoked paprika** — ½ tsp — 0
- **Garlic** — 2 medium clove(s), grated — 0
- **Uncooked boneless skinless chicken breast(s)** — 1 pound(s), cut into bite-sized pieces — 0
- **Yellow pepper(s)** — 1 small, sliced — 0
- **Sweet red pepper(s)** — 1 small, sliced — 0
- **Uncooked red onion(s)** — ½ large, vertically sliced — 0
- **Romaine lettuce** — 4 leaf/leaves — 0
- **Whole wheat pita(s)** — 4 pita(s) — 17
- **Tzatziki (cucumber yogurt sauce)** — 6 Tbsp — 3

Instructions

1. Place a sheet pan in the oven and preheat the oven to 425°F (leave the pan in the oven).

2. In a medium bowl, whisk together the yogurt, lemon juice, 1 tbsp oil, cumin, oregano, ½ tsp each salt and pepper, smoked paprika, and garlic. Add the chicken and toss well to coat. Marinate at room temperature for 10 minutes.

3. Meanwhile, in a large bowl, toss together the bell peppers, onion, remaining 1 tbsp oil, and remaining ¼ tsp each salt and pepper.

4. Carefully remove the hot pan from the oven and coat with cooking spray. Arrange the chicken mixture on one side of the pan and the onion mixture on the other side. Bake until the chicken is cooked through and the vegetables are tender, about 20 minutes, stirring after 10 minutes.

5. Remove the pan from the oven and preheat the broiler to High. If there is liquid on the pan, soak it up with paper towels. Broil the mixture until lightly charred, 2 to 4 minutes. Arrange 1 lettuce leaf in each pita; divide the chicken and vegetables evenly among the pitas. Spoon 1 ½ tbsp tzatziki over each pita.

Rice Noodle Chicken Lettuce Wraps

6

Total Time: 0:15 **Prep:** 0:10 **Cook:** 0:05 **Serves:** 4 **Difficulty:** Easy

This five-ingredient recipe comes together in a flash and is almost no-cook; you just have to boil some water. Convenient broccoli slaw, rotisserie chicken, and bottled peanut sauce take away almost all of the prep work while building serious flavor. The noodle mixture tastes fresh, offers lots of crunch, and delivers plenty of protein.

Ingredients

Uncooked thin rice vermicelli noodles — 10
3 oz

Broccoli slaw — 0
3 cup(s)

Skinless original seasoning rotisserie chicken breast — 0
8 oz, shredded

Canned Thai peanut sauce — 13
½ cup(s)

Lettuce — 0
12 leaf/leaves, large, Boston or butter leaves suggested

Instructions

1. Bring 3 cups of water to a boil. Place the noodles in a medium bowl; pour the boiling water over the noodles. Allow the mixture to stand until the noodles are al dente, 5 to 7 minutes.

2. Drain the noodles and rinse with cold water; drain well. Snip the noodles a few times with kitchen shears. In a large bowl, combine the noodles, broccoli slaw, chicken, and peanut sauce; toss well to coat. Spoon about ½ cup of the noodle mixture into each lettuce leaf.

3. Serving size: 3 lettuce wraps

Chicken vindaloo

Total Time: 1:00 **Prep:** 0:15 **Cook:** 0:25 **Serves:** 4 **Difficulty:** Easy

Vindaloo is known to be a fiery Indian dish, redolent with complex spices and vinegar tang underneath the heat. If you seed the serrano pepper, you'll end up with a medium-spicy dish. For a mild dish, seed the serrano and reduce the amount of cayenne pepper to ¼ teaspoon. To go all in on the heat, leave the seeds in the serrano and use the full amount of cayenne pepper. If the finished dish ends up a little too spicy for you, serve with a cooling dollop of plain Greek yogurt.

Ingredients

- **White vinegar** — ¼ cup(s) — 0
- **Paprika** — 1 tsp — 0
- **Kosher salt** — 1 tsp, divided — 0
- **Ginger root** — 1 tsp, peeled and grated — 0
- **Dried ground coriander** — ½ tsp — 0
- **Ground cumin** — ½ tsp — 0
- **Cayenne pepper** — ½ tsp — 0
- **Ground cinnamon** — ¼ tsp — 0
- **Garlic** — 4 medium clove(s), grated — 0
- **Uncooked boneless skinless chicken breast** — 1 pound(s), cut into bite-sized pieces — 0
- **Canola oil** — 1 Tbsp — 4
- **Uncooked onion(s)** — 1 cup(s), chopped — 0
- **Serrano chile(s)** — 1 item(s), seeded if desired and minced — 0
- **Canned unsalted tomato paste** — 1 Tbsp — 0
- **Cilantro** — ¼ cup(s), chopped — 0
- **Cooked basmati rice** — 2 cup(s) — 13

Instructions

1. In a medium bowl, whisk the vinegar, paprika, ½ tsp salt, ginger, coriander, cumin, cayenne, cinnamon, and garlic. Add the chicken to the bowl and toss well to coat. Marinate at room temperature for 20 minutes.

2. Heat the oil in a large skillet over medium heat. Add the onion and serrano pepper; cook until the onion softens, about 5 minutes. Add the tomato paste; cook 1 minute, stirring constantly. Stir in ½ cup water and remaining ½ tsp salt, scraping the bottom of the pan to loosen the browned bits. Stir in the chicken mixture and marinade. Bring to a boil. Reduce the heat, cover, and simmer until the chicken is done, about 15 minutes. Sprinkle the chicken mixture with cilantro. Serve with rice.

3. Serving size: ½ cup rice and about ⅔ cup chicken mixture

Spicy breaded chicken sandwich

Total Time: 0:50 **Prep:** 0:15 **Cook:** 0:20 **Serves:** 4 **Difficulty:** Easy

Our version of this fast-food favorite starts the same way as its restaurant counterpart: by brining the chicken in dill pickle juice. Since we do a quick soak of just 15 minutes, we pierce the chicken all over with a fork so the brine can more quickly penetrate with its tangy-salty flavor. A bit of baking powder in the breading makes it puff up and crisp as the chicken bakes. A good bit of cayenne pepper brings the heat level in at medium-hot. For medium heat, decrease the amount to ¾ teaspoon, or for a mild version, go to ¼ to ½ teaspoon.

Ingredients

- **Cooking spray** — 4 spray(s) — 0
- **Uncooked boneless skinless chicken breast(s)** — 1 pound(s), 4 (4-oz) cutlets — 0
- **Pickle juice** — 4 fl oz, dill (1/2 cup) — 0
- **Low-fat milk** — ¼ cup(s) — 1
- **Egg(s)** — 1 large egg(s) — 0
- **All-purpose flour** — ⅔ cup(s) — 9
- **Cornstarch** — 1 Tbsp — 1
- **Cayenne pepper** — 1 tsp — 0
- **Baking powder** — ¾ tsp — 0
- **Paprika** — ¾ tsp — 0
- **Chili powder** — ¾ tsp — 0
- **Garlic powder** — ¾ tsp — 0
- **Table salt** — ½ tsp — 0
- **Canola oil** — 2 Tbsp — 8
- **Unsweetened dill pickle(s)** — 8 chip(s) — 0
- **Light hamburger bun(s)** — 4 bun(s), toasted — 9

Instructions

1. Place a sheet pan in the oven and preheat the oven to 425°F.

2. Pierce the chicken all over with a fork. Place the chicken in a zip-top plastic bag (or glass container with lid). Add the pickle juice, seal the bag (or cover the container), and shake to combine. Marinate at room temperature for 15 minutes, shaking occasionally.

3. Meanwhile, in a shallow dish, whisk together the milk and egg. In another shallow bowl, whisk together the flour, cornstarch, cayenne pepper, baking powder, paprika, chili powder, garlic powder, and salt. Working with 1 chicken cutlet at a time, lightly dredge the chicken in the flour mixture, shaking off the excess. Dip the chicken in the egg mixture, turning to coat. Return the chicken to the flour mixture, turning to coat and gently pressing to help the flour mixture adhere.

4. Carefully remove the hot pan from the oven. Coat the pan with cooking spray and drizzle with the oil. Arrange the breaded chicken on the hot pan. Bake until browned and crisped on the bottom, about 10 minutes. Using a thin spatula, carefully turn the chicken over; bake until browned and crisped on the bottom, 8 to 10 minutes. Arrange 2 pickle chips and 1 chicken cutlet in each hamburger bun.

Drunken noodles with chicken

Total Time: 0:30 **Prep:** 0:15 **Cook:** 0:15 **Serves:** 4 **Difficulty:** Easy

This dish is thought to get its name from the notion that it's especially appreciated after you've had a few drinks. If you want the dish to be mild, be sure to seed the jalapeños. For medium heat, leave the seeds in one pepper, and for a more fiery flavor, leave the seeds in both. Though not traditional, we've added some zucchini to add some color and extra nutrition.

Ingredients

Dry rice noodles — 25
8 oz, wide variety, straight cut

Uncooked boneless skinless chicken breast — 0
1 pound(s), thinly sliced

Asian fish sauce — 0
1 Tbsp

Uncooked scallion(s) — 0
10 medium

Toasted sesame oil — 7
1 ½ Tbsp

Uncooked zucchini — 0
2 cup(s), sliced, sliced into half moons

Garlic — 0
4 large clove(s), minced

Jalapeño pepper(s) — 0
2 medium, seeded if desired and minced

Oyster sauce — 1
2 Tbsp

Low sodium soy sauce — 0
1 Tbsp

Basil — 0
1 cup(s), Thai or sweet, large leaves torn

Instructions

1. Cook noodles according to package directions; drain and rinse with cold water. Drain well.

2. Meanwhile, in a medium bowl toss chicken with fish sauce. Cut scallions into ½-inch slices, separating white and light green parts from dark green parts.

3. Heat oil in a wok or large skillet over medium-high heat. Add chicken mixture to pan; sauté until just starting to brown, about 3 minutes. Add white and light green scallion pieces, zucchini, garlic, and jalapeño; sauté until chicken is cooked through and zucchini is crisp-tender, about 5 minutes. Add noodles, oyster sauce, soy sauce, and dark green scallion pieces; cook, tossing constantly, until heated through, about 2 minutes. Stir in basil.

4. Serving size: about 2 cups

Lemony chicken francaise

Total Time: 0:30   **Prep:** 0:15   **Cook:** 0:15   **Serves:** 4   **Difficulty:** Easy

With a tangy, buttery citrus-wine sauce, these breaded chicken cutlets will perk up any weeknight. The chicken is pounded thin, dredged in flour, and coated in beaten egg, then cooked in a skillet. Because the eggy mixture is on the outside, the chicken takes on a pretty golden color, and the breading ends up with a hearty, rich texture similar to a crepe.

Ingredients

Cooking spray — 0
4 spray(s)

Uncooked boneless skinless chicken breast(s) — 0
20 oz (4 [5-oz] cutlets)

Kosher salt — 0
¾ tsp, divided

Garlic powder — 0
½ tsp

Black pepper — 0
¼ tsp

All-purpose flour — 3
¼ cup(s), divided

Egg(s) — 0
2 large egg(s), lightly beaten

No-salt-added chicken stock — 0
⅔ cup(s)

White wine — 2
⅓ cup(s)

Fresh lemon juice — 0
2 Tbsp

Lemon(s) — 0
½ item(s), thinly sliced

Unsalted butter — 6
1 Tbsp

Fresh parsley — 0
2 Tbsp, chopped

Instructions

1. Working with one cutlet at a time, place the chicken between two sheets of plastic wrap; pound to a ¼-inch thickness. Arrange the pounded cutlets in a single layer on a work surface or a large piece of plastic wrap. Sprinkle the chicken evenly with ½ tsp salt, garlic powder, and black pepper. Sprinkle the top of the chicken with 1 ½ tbsp flour, rubbing gently to coat; turn the chicken over, sprinkle with 1 ½ tbsp flour, and rub gently to coat. Place the eggs in a pie plate or other shallow dish; dip the chicken in the egg, turning to coat.

2. Coat a large nonstick skillet with cooking spray and heat over medium. Add 2 cutlets to the pan; cook until lightly browned and cooked through, about 3 minutes per side. Remove from the pan and repeat with the remaining 2 cutlets. Wipe the skillet clean with paper towels.

3. In a 2-cup glass measuring cup or medium bowl, whisk together the chicken stock, wine, lemon juice, and remaining 1 tbsp flour. Pour the mixture into the skillet and bring to a boil over medium, stirring frequently. Stir in the remaining ¼ tsp salt and lemon slices; cook until the sauce thickens, 2 to 3 minutes. Stir in the butter. Add the chicken to the pan, turning to coat with the sauce. Sprinkle with the parsley.

Chicken zucchini boats ③

Total Time: 1:05 **Prep:** 0:20 **Cook:** 0:45 **Serves:** 4 **Difficulty:** Easy

Looking for dinner inspiration? Turn to these South-of-the-border-inspired stuffed zucchini boats that are rich in flavor thanks to seasoned tomato sauce and a Mexican cheese blend. You can assemble the zucchini in a baking dish ahead of time and pop them in the oven right before serving—just extend the bake time by about 10 minutes. We used chopped fresh basil as a garnish, but you could use chopped fresh cilantro, green onions, or even parsley if you'd like. Serve with chips, guacamole and salsa, or a roasted vegetable soup spiked with cilantro. Summer squash can be used instead of the zucchini, if you prefer, and leftover cooked turkey breast can be swapped for the chicken.

Ingredients

Cooking spray — 0
4 spray(s), divided

Canned tomato sauce — 0
2 cup(s), with basil, garlic and oregano, divided

Uncooked zucchini — 0
4 medium

Olive oil — 1
1 tsp

Cooked skinless boneless chicken breast(s) — 0
2 ½ cup(s), chopped, or shredded (homemade or store-bought)

WW Reduced fat shredded Mexican style blend cheese — 9
1 cup(s)

Basil — 0
1 Tbsp, chopped

Instructions

1. Preheat oven to 375°F. Coat a 9- X 13-inch casserole dish with cooking spray; spread 1/2 cup tomato sauce in bottom of dish.

2. Trim zucchini; slice each zucchini in half lengthwise. Using a spoon or a melon baller, remove flesh from center of each zucchini half. Chop scooped out zucchini flesh; set aside. Place zucchini halves in a single layer in prepared dish.

3. Heat oil in a large sauté pan over medium heat; add chopped zucchini and cook, stirring, about 3 minutes. Add remaining tomato sauce and chicken to pan; cook, stirring, 1 minute. Divide chicken mixture among zucchini halves; cover pan with aluminum foil.

4. Bake 30 minutes; remove aluminum foil and sprinkle with cheese. Bake, uncovered, until cheese is melted, 3-5 minutes. Remove from oven; garnish with chopped basil.

5. Serving size: 2 zucchini boats

Slow Cooker Chicken Tinga Tacos ④

Total Time: 4:25   **Prep:** 0:20   **Cook:** 4:05   **Serves:** 8   **Difficulty:** Easy

Boneless, skinless chicken breasts slow cook to shreddable tenderness in a spicy, smoky, chipotle-spiked sauce. It's just enough sauce to coat the shredded chicken so that it's not swimming in excess liquid. As the chicken cooks in the slow cooker, you'll make pickled red onions for the tacos. They're beautifully jewel-like and incredibly easy to prepare.

Ingredients

- **Olive oil** — 1 Tbsp — ④
- **Uncooked onion(s)** — 1 medium, white or yellow, thinly sliced — 0
- **Garlic** — 5 medium clove(s), minced — 0
- **Uncooked boneless skinless chicken breast(s)** — 2 pound(s) — 0
- **No-salt-added canned tomato sauce** — 8 oz — 0
- **Canned chipotle peppers in adobo sauce** — 2 Tbsp, chopped — 0
- **Kosher salt** — 1 ¼ tsp, divided — 0
- **Ground cumin** — 1 tsp — 0
- **Dried oregano** — ¾ tsp — 0
- **Smoked paprika** — ½ tsp — 0
- **Bay leaf** — 2 leaf/leaves — 0
- **Cider vinegar** — ¾ cup(s) — 0
- **Uncooked red onion(s)** — 1 ½ cup(s), sliced, vertically sliced — 0
- **Avocado** — 1 medium, sliced — ⑧
- **Cotija cheese** — ½ cup(s), crumbled — ⑧
- **Cilantro** — ½ cup(s), sprigs (optional) — 0
- **Corn tortilla(s)** — 8 medium — ⑫

Instructions

1. Heat the oil in a medium skillet over medium-high heat. Add the white or yellow onion and garlic; sauté until softened and lightly browned, about 5 minutes. Spoon the onion mixture into the bottom of a slow cooker. Top with the chicken.

2. In a medium bowl, stir together the tomato sauce, chipotle, 1 tsp salt, cumin, oregano, paprika, and bay leaves. Pour the mixture over the chicken. Cover and cook on Low until the chicken is tender, 3 to 4 hours.

3. Meanwhile, combine the vinegar and ¾ cup water in a small saucepan; bring to a boil. Add the red onion and return the liquid to a boil. Immediately remove the pan from the heat and let stand until the mixture cools to room temperature. Drain the onions and place in a bowl; stir in the remaining ¼ tsp salt.

4. When the chicken is tender, shred the meat in the slow cooker, stirring it with the sauce to combine. Divide the chicken, pickled onions, avocado, cheese, and cilantro evenly over the tortillas.

Grilled Sesame-Garlic Chicken Breasts

0

Total Time: 0:15 Prep: 0:05 Cook: 0:10 Serves: 4 Difficulty: Easy

The tasty seasoning blend here combines garlic, sesame seeds, tamari, salt, and black pepper in one convenient ingredient that deliciously lends a little Asian flair to simple grilled chicken breasts. We grill lemon slices alongside the chicken for a perky and pretty garnish, but you can omit them if you don't have any on hand; or try grilled orange or tangerine slices for a sweeter flavor that also pairs well with the sesame and garlic.

Ingredients

Cooking spray — 0
4 spray(s)

Uncooked boneless skinless chicken breast(s) — 0
1 pound(s)(4 [4-oz] breasts)

Dried seasoning mix — 0
2 tsp, sesame-garlic variety

Lemon(s) — 0
4 slice(s)

Instructions

1. Prepare an outdoor grill to medium-high heat or heat a large grill pan over medium-high.

2. Coat both sides of the chicken breasts with cooking spray; sprinkle both sides of the chicken evenly with the seasoning blend. Arrange the chicken and lemon slices on the grill rack or grill pan; close the grill lid, or tent the grill pan with foil. Grill the chicken until it is cooked through, 4 to 5 minutes per side. Grill the lemon slices until grill marks appear, about 2 minutes per side. Top each chicken breast with 1 lemon slice.

3. Serving size: 1 chicken breast

Easy Thai chicken veggie bowl

Total Time: 0:05   Prep: 0:05   Cook: -   Serves: 1   Difficulty: Easy

Here's a great way to make use of small amounts of leftover foods. A modest half-cup of cooked sweet potatoes, edamame, and chicken, plus a handful of fresh broccoli slaw, come together for an easy lunch or dinner you can pull together in a flash. Purchased Thai peanut sauce is enlivened with a simple spritz of lime for perky, bold notes. You can serve with additional lime wedges for more zip.

Ingredients

Canned Thai peanut sauce — 3
2 Tbsp

Fresh lime juice — 0
2 tsp

Broccoli slaw — 0
1 cup(s)

Cooked shredded chicken breast — 0
½ cup(s)

Edamame (shelled) — 0
½ cup(s)

Cooked sweet potato(es) — 2
½ cup(s), cubed

Instructions

1 In a medium bowl, whisk together the peanut sauce and lime juice. Add the broccoli slaw and chicken; toss to coat. In a shallow bowl, arrange the edamame and sweet potatoes; top with the chicken mixture.

2 Serving size: 1 bowl

Confetti chicken chili by Ross Mathews

Total Time: 1:00 **Prep:** 0:20 **Cook:** 0:40 **Serves:** 8 **Difficulty:** Easy

Warm up with this chicken chili on cold winter days. Ross serves it with a spoonful of low-fat sour cream, some chopped scallions, a lime wedge, and a few shakes of hot sauce. Other great garnishes include nonfat plain yogurt, low-fat shredded cheese, tortilla strips, and/or thinly sliced radishes. Freeze any leftovers in pint-size containers for easy, reheatable meals another day.

Ingredients

Olive oil — 4
1 Tbsp

Uncooked boneless skinless chicken breast — 0
1 pound(s), cut into ½-inch cubes

Kosher salt — 0
2 pinch(es)

Black pepper — 0
2 pinch(es)

Uncooked onion(s) — 0
1 medium, yellow variety, chopped finely

Yellow pepper(s) — 0
1 medium, chopped finely

Sweet red pepper(s) — 0
1 medium, chopped finely

Garlic clove — 0
2 clove(s), chopped finely

Crushed red pepper flakes — 0
2 pinch(es)

Canned white beans — 0
30 oz, rinsed and drained

Canned low-sodium chicken broth — 1
29 fl oz

Canned green chile peppers — 0
4 oz, mild variety, diced

Fresh lime(s) — 0
1 medium

Uncooked scallion(s) — 0
4 medium, sliced thinly

Reduced-fat sour cream — 10
½ cup(s)

Hot sauce — 0
8 splash(es), optional

Instructions

1. In a large soup pot, warm oil over medium-high heat. Add chicken, salt, and pepper; sauté chicken until lightly browned, about 1 to 2 minutes. Add onion and bell peppers; sauté until vegetables begin to soften, about 3 to 4 minutes.

2. Add garlic and crushed red pepper; cook, stirring frequently, 1 to 2 minutes. Add beans, broth, and chiles; squeeze lime juice into pot, stir, and bring to a boil. Reduce heat to low and simmer, covered, stirring often, about 30 minutes.

3. Taste and adjust seasonings, if necessary. Serve topped with sour cream, scallions, lime wedges, and optional hot sauce.

4. Serving size: about 1 cup chili and 1 tbsp sour cream

Easy Chicken Taco Bowl

Total Time: 0:10 **Prep:** 0:10 **Cook:** - **Serves:** 4 **Difficulty:** Easy

Sometimes, the best busy-day, time-is-tight meals are ones that you assemble instead of cook. Here's a great example: a rice bowl that you build from convenience foods—precooked rice, rotisserie chicken, packaged coleslaw mix, and salsa. Of course, creamy avocado is the perfect finishing touch. Since all of the seasoning comes from the salsa (which you'll mix in when you're ready to eat), choose one that delivers the flavors you love, from spicy to mild to tangy to roasty. Serve the rice and chicken chilled, heated, or at room temperature.

Ingredients

Cooked long grain brown rice
2 cup(s)

Skinless original seasoning rotisserie chicken breast
12 oz, shredded

Packaged coleslaw mix (shredded cabbage and carrots)
4 cup(s)

Avocado
2 medium, sliced

Salsa, restaurant type
1 cup(s)

Instructions

1. Into each of 4 large, shallow bowls, arrange ½ cup rice, 3 oz chicken, 1 cup coleslaw mix, and ½ an avocado. Top each serving with 1/4 cup salsa.

2. Serving size: 1 bowl

Slow cooker chicken taco soup

Total Time: 6:05 **Prep:** 0:05 **Cook:** 6:00 **Serves:** 6 **Difficulty:** Easy

Slow cooker recipes that require lots of prep (tons of chopping and/or browning or sautéing) undermine the convenience promised by the appliance. So this recipe delivers ultimate ease with no chopping or browning—just stir everything together in the cooker (no need to thaw the veggies) and let it go. At the end, you'll shred the chicken, which takes almost no time.

Ingredients

Frozen corn kernels — 0
2 cup(s)

Frozen pepper strips — 0
1 ½ cup(s)

Frozen chopped onions — 0
⅔ cup(s)

Chili powder — 1
2 Tbsp

Ground cumin — 0
1 Tbsp

Garlic powder — 1
1 Tbsp

Table salt — 0
½ tsp

Salsa tatemada (roasted tomato salsa) — 1
16 oz

Canned kidney beans — 0
15 oz, rinsed and drained

Uncooked boneless skinless chicken thigh(s) — 17
1 ½ pound(s)

Shredded reduced-fat Mexican-style cheese — 5
6 Tbsp

Cilantro — 0
2 Tbsp, leaves (optional)

Instructions

1. In a slow cooker, combine the corn, pepper strips, onions, chili powder, cumin, garlic, salt, salsa, and beans. Stir in 2 cups water and the chicken thighs. Cover and cook on Low until the chicken is very tender, 6 to 7 hours.

2. Remove the chicken from the slow cooker; shred the meat with 2 forks and stir back into the soup. Ladle the soup into bowls; top with the cheese and cilantro, if desired.

3. Serving size: 1 ⅔ cups

Gravy Chicken by Palak Palel

Total Time: 0:45   Prep: 0:10   Cook: 0:35   Serves: 4   Difficulty: Easy

This recipe may require a trip to your local South Asian grocery store to get Shan's Nihari seasoning mix, but it'll be well-worth it (you can also order it online). It adds a unique mix of salt and spice that are complemented so well by the cumin, garlic, and turmeric in this recipe. Enjoy this dish on its own or over regular or cauliflower rice to sop up the delicious gravy. We made it with chicken breasts but it would also work with chicken thighs.

Ingredients

Uncooked boneless skinless chicken breast — 0
1 ½ pound(s), cut into bite-size pieces

Shan Nihari seasoning mix — 1
3 Tbsp, divided

Vegetable oil — 14
3 Tbsp

Cumin seeds — 0
1 tsp

Uncooked onion(s) — 0
2 large, thinly sliced

Minced garlic — 0
3 Tbsp

Canned tomato paste — 1
2 Tbsp

Ground turmeric — 0
¼ tsp

Water — 0
1 ½ cup(s)

Cilantro — 0
1 cup(s), chopped

Instructions

1. Sprinkle chicken with 1 tbsp Shan Nihari and set aside.

2. Heat a large pot over medium heat and add oil. Once oil is hot, add cumin seeds and let them cook for a few seconds until they start to sputter.

3. Add onions and cook, stirring often, until they are very soft, about 15 minutes. Add garlic, tomato paste, and turmeric, and cook, stirring often, about 2 to 3 minutes.

4. Stir in remaining 2 tbsp Shan Nihari spice mix and slowly pour in water in small additions, stirring after each addition (the sauce will thicken after each pour).

5. Add reserved chicken to pot and stir well. Reduce heat to low, cover pot with a tight-fitting lid, and let cook until chicken is cooked through, 15 to 20 minutes.

6. Uncover pot, stir in cilantro, and serve hot.

7. Serving size: about 1 cup

Chicken prosciutt-OMG by Ross Mathews

Total Time: 1:00 **Prep:** 0:20 **Cook:** 0:40 **Serves:** 2 **Difficulty:** Easy

This Italian-inspired recipe is nice and versatile—experiment with different vegetables every time you make it. Swap out the spinach for whatever veggies you have on hand such as chopped broccoli, zucchini or mushrooms. Just make sure to let the chicken cool for about 5 minutes after taking it out of the oven (to let the cheese firm up).

Ingredients

Fresh baby spinach
4 cup(s)

Basil
2 Tbsp, torn into small pieces

Kosher salt
2 pinch(es), divided

Black pepper
2 pinch(es), divided

Garlic powder
1 pinch(es)

Crushed red pepper flakes
1 pinch(es)

Lemon(s)
½ medium

Uncooked boneless skinless chicken breast
½ pound(s), 2 (4 oz) pieces

Plum tomato(es)
1 medium, ends trimmed, cut into 4 rounds

Semisoft goat cheese
1 oz, from a log, cut into 4 rounds

Prosciutto
2 slice(s)

Instructions

1. Preheat oven 425°F. Line a small baking pan with parchment paper (or aluminum foil coated with cooking spray).

2. Set a medium nonstick skillet over medium heat. Add spinach, basil, and 1 pinch each salt, pepper, garlic powder, and crushed red pepper; squeeze lemon juice over top. Cook, stirring, until spinach wilts, about 1 to 2 minutes; set aside.

3. Place chicken on a cutting board. Working with one breast at a time, slice horizontally almost all the way, but not through, each breast. Open breasts so they lay flat like an open book and place 2 tomato slices on one side of each breast; sprinkle tomatoes with a pinch each salt and pepper. Divide spinach mixture over tomatoes and top each with 2 slices goat cheese; close breasts and carefully wrap a prosciutto slice around each one.

4. Place chicken on prepared pan. Bake until an internal temperature of 165°F and prosciutto is nice and crispy, about 35 to 40 minutes.

5. Serving size: 1 chicken breast

Chapter 4:
Soup & Stew

Turkey meatball and escarole soup

Total Time: 4:35 **Prep:** 0:35 **Cook:** 4:00 **Serves:** 8 **Difficulty:** Easy

Soaking torn bread in milk before adding it to the turkey mixture ensures the meatballs stay moist and tender after hours in the slow cooker, while Parmesan adds a touch of classic Italian flavor. Mix lightly and shape the meatballs gently to keep them from becoming too dense. Option: Add 1 cup of sliced white mushrooms or earthy cremini mushrooms to the soup along with the meatballs in step 4.

Ingredients

Whole wheat bread — 4
2 slice(s), crust removed and cut into 1/2-inch pieces

Reduced-sodium chicken broth — 2
8 cup(s), or 2 (32-ounce) cartons

Low-fat milk — 1
¼ cup(s)

Uncooked 99% fat-free ground turkey breast — 0
1 ¼ pound(s)

Grated Parmesan cheese — 4
¼ cup(s)

Egg(s) — 0
1 large egg(s), lightly beaten

Uncooked shallot(s) — 0
1 large, minced

Fresh parsley — 0
3 Tbsp, flat leaf, chopped, divided

Table salt — 0
1 tsp

Black pepper — 0
½ tsp

Extra virgin olive oil — 4
1 Tbsp

Escarole — 0
4 cup(s), Swiss chard or kale, thinly sliced leaves, lightly packed

Canned cannellini beans — 0
15 ½ oz, rinsed and drained

Instructions

1. Mix together bread and milk in large bowl; let stand until softened, about 5 minutes. Add turkey, Parmesan, egg, shallot, 2 tbsp parsley, salt, and pepper, stirring until mixed well but not overmixed.

2. With damp hands, shape turkey mixture into 24 meatballs, using about 2 tbsp for each meatball; transfer meatballs to sheet of foil as they are shaped. Wash bowl.

3. Heat oil in large heavy nonstick skillet over medium-high heat. Add meatballs, in two batches, and cook until well browned, about 5 minutes per batch. Transfer meatballs to cleaned bowl as they are browned.

4. Combine broth, escarole, and beans in 5- or 6-quart slow cooker; add meatballs. Cover and cook until meatballs are cooked through, about 4 hours on Low. Serve soup sprinkled with remaining 1 tbsp parsley.

5. Serving size: 1 1/3 cups soup and 3 meatballs

Ginger meatball and vegetable soup

Total Time: 0:25 **Prep:** 0:15 **Cook:** 0:10 **Serves:** 6 **Difficulty:** Easy

These gingery meatballs are a snap to make—you just drop them from a tablespoon onto the broiler rack. While the meatballs cook, the veggies simmer, so it's a one-pot meal that tastes like it took much longer to make. Use a melon ball to scoop the meat mixture and shape them into evenly-sized meatballs. Roll the meat into balls using the palm of your hands. Stand near the sink or keep a small bowl of water nearby in case the meat starts to stick to your hands, you can quickly wet your hands to prevent this.

Ingredients

- **Cooking spray** — 1 spray(s)
- **Chili garlic sauce** — 1 tsp
- **Uncooked 99% fat-free ground turkey breast** — 1 pound(s)
- **Uncooked shallot(s)** — 1 medium, minced
- **Egg white(s)** — 1 large
- **Ginger root** — 4 tsp, fresh grated
- **Cilantro** — ¼ cup(s), fresh, chopped
- **Table salt** — ½ tsp, or to taste
- **Black pepper** — ¼ tsp
- **Canned chicken broth** — 6 cup(s)
- **Shredded uncooked napa cabbage** — 4 cup(s)
- **Uncooked carrot(s)** — 2 medium, cut into thin strips
- **Uncooked bell pepper(s)** — 1 item(s), small, red variety, cut into thin strips
- **Fresh lime juice** — 1 Tbsp
- **Asian fish sauce** — 1 Tbsp
- **Uncooked scallion(s)** — 2 medium, thinly sliced

Instructions

1. Spray broiler rack with nonstick spray. Preheat broiler.

2. Stir together turkey, shallot, egg white, 2 teaspoons ginger, the cilantro, salt, and pepper in large bowl. Drop mixture by tablespoonfuls onto prepared broiler rack. Broil 5 inches from heat, turning once, until cooked through, about 8 minutes. Set aside.

3. Meanwhile, combine broth, chili-garlic sauce, and remaining 2 teaspoons ginger in Dutch oven. Bring to boil over medium-high heat. Add cabbage, carrots, and bell pepper and return to boil. Reduce heat to medium-low and simmer until vegetables are crisp-tender, about 5 minutes. Remove from heat and gently stir in meatballs, lime juice, and fish sauce.

4. Ladle evenly into 6 bowls and sprinkle with scallions.

5. Serving size: about 1 1/2 cups

Peanut Stew with Spinach & Sweet Potatoes

4

Total Time: 1:11   Prep: 0:23   Cook: 0:48   Serves: 6   Difficulty: Easy

This vegan, Senegalese stew makes a rich and comforting winter warmer. Creamy peanut butter thickens the soup with a deeply flavorful nuttiness that plays well against the sweetness of the sweet potatoes and the spice of the cayenne. I doubt your guests will miss the meat as this combination of ingredients makes this dish super hearty and filling. This one-dish meal needs no accompaniment but a light and crunchy green salad with a simple vinaigrette will amp the veggie presence for your dinner. Pack in a thermos for a hot and tasty lunch on the go. This dish makes a great starter for a dinner party. Divide your servings in half so your guests aren't full before the main course is served. Then you have 12 servings in only an hour of work.

Ingredients

Cooking spray — 0
1 spray(s)

Uncooked onion(s) — 0
2 medium, roughly chopped

Green pepper(s) — 0
1 medium, cored and roughly chopped

Uncooked sweet potato(es) — 5
½ pound(s), peeled and chopped into 1/2-inch cubes

Uncooked carrot(s) — 0
2 medium, peeled and thinly sliced

Garlic — 0
2 medium clove(s), minced

Ginger root — 0
2 Tbsp, fresh, minced

Ground cloves — 0
½ tsp

Table salt — 0
½ tsp

Cayenne pepper — 0
¼ tsp

Vegetable broth — 1
4 cup(s), reduced-sodium

Reduced sodium peanut butter — 18
6 Tbsp, natural, creamy-variety

Fresh spinach — 0
8 cup(s), leaves, stemmed, packed, chopped

Instructions

1. Coat a large saucepan with cooking spray and set over medium heat. Add onion and bell pepper; cook, stirring often, until softened, about 3 minutes.

2. Stir in the sweet potato, carrots and garlic; cook for 1 minute, stirring often. Add the ginger, cloves, salt and cayenne; cook for 30 seconds.

3. Pour in the vegetable broth and bring to a simmer, scraping up any browned bits from the bottom of the pan. Stir in the peanut butter until smooth.

4. Cover, reduce the heat to low, and simmer slowly, stirring once in a while, until the sweet potatoes are tender, about 30 minutes.

5. Add the spinach; cook, stirring occasionally, for 10 minutes. Yields about 1 2/3 cups per serving.

Chipotle-Black Bean Chili 0

Total Time: 0:17 **Prep:** 0:10 **Cook:** 0:07 **Serves:** 1 **Difficulty:** Easy

Usually, chili recipes require quite a bit of work, maybe a crock-pot, and definitely a lot of people to eat their massive yield. But this recipe for chipotle-black bean chili keeps it simple. To make it, all you need is 17 minutes, and one hungry person since it produces just a single serving! You just combine the six ingredients in a bowl and pop 'em in the microwave; it doesn't get much simpler than that! And really, what's better than a one-step recipe? When you're done creating this rich, hearty dish, top it with some optional fresh lime for touch of acidity.

Ingredients

Canned diced tomatoes 0
1 cup(s), fire-roasted variety

Yellow pepper(s) 0
½ medium, chopped

Canned black beans 0
½ cup(s), rinsed and drained

Canned chipotle peppers in adobo sauce 0
½ tsp, or more to taste

Chili powder 0
1 tsp

Cilantro 0
2 Tbsp, fresh, chopped

Instructions

1. Combine all ingredients, except cilantro, in a microwave-safe bowl; cover and microwave on high until peppers are tender, 7 minutes. Stir in cilantro.

2. Makes 1 serving.

Creamy Tomato-Basil Soup ②

Total Time: 0:25 **Prep:** 0:10 **Cook:** 0:15 **Serves:** 4 **Difficulty:** Easy

This soup serves up restaurant-quality looks. But its velvety texture comes from canned white beans and sautéed onions. Fresh basil tops off the fanciness. Stash veggie trimmings (from carrots, tomatoes, celery, or herbs) in the freezer to make your own veggie stock anytime. Toss the frozen scraps into a pot and cover them with water. Bring to a boil, then simmer for 30 minutes. Strain out the solids and, boom, homemade stock.

Ingredients

Olive oil — 9
2 Tbsp

Uncooked onion(s) — 0
1 ½ cup(s), chopped

Fat free reduced sodium vegetable broth — 0
1 cup(s)

Canned diced tomatoes — 0
29 oz, undrained (2 [14.5-oz] cans)

Canned great northern beans — 0
1 ½ cup(s), drained and rinsed (1 [15-oz] can)

Kosher salt — 0
½ tsp, plus more to taste

Black pepper — 0
½ tsp, plus more for garnish

Basil — 0
½ cup(s), chopped, plus more for garnish

Instructions

1. In a medium saucepan, heat the oil over medium. Add the onion; cook, stirring occasionally, until almost tender, about 8 minutes. Add the stock, tomatoes with juices, beans, salt, and black pepper. Increase heat to medium-high. Bring to a boil and cook for 5 minutes. Stir in the basil.

2. Transfer the soup to a blender and purée until smooth. (Or, using an immersion blender, purée the soup in the pot.) Season to taste with salt and black pepper. Divide the soup among 4 bowls. Garnish with more basil and black pepper.

3. Serving size: about 1⅓ cups

Turkey Minestrone

Total Time: 0:40 **Prep:** 0:15 **Cook:** 0:25 **Serves:** 4 **Difficulty:** Easy

Minestrone is an Italian soup made with vegetables, beans, and pasta. Typically, it doesn't include meat, but we added crumbled meatloaves to make this soup even heartier. If you don't have ditalini, feel free to use elbow macaroni instead.

Ingredients

Canola oil — 4
1 Tbsp

Uncooked onion(s) — 0
½ cup(s), chopped

Uncooked carrot(s) — 0
½ cup(s), thinly sliced

Uncooked celery — 0
⅓ cup(s), thinly sliced

Garlic — 0
2 medium clove(s), finely chopped

No-salt-added chicken stock — 1
3 cup(s)

No salt added diced tomatoes — 0
14 ½ oz

Canned low sodium red kidney beans — 0
15 oz, rinsed and drained

Kosher salt — 0
½ tsp

Italian seasoning — 0
½ tsp

Uncooked ditalini pasta — 5
2 oz, a scant ½ cup

Uncooked zucchini — 0
1 medium, chopped

Muffin-Pan Turkey Meatloaves — 2
3 item(s), crumbled (search for the recipe in the WW app)

Instructions

1. In a large saucepan, heat the oil over medium-high. Add the onion, carrot, celery, and garlic and cook for 3 minutes, stirring occasionally. Stir in the broth, tomatoes, beans, salt, and Italian seasoning and bring to a boil, occasionally stirring and scraping up any browned bits from the bottom of the pan.

2. Add the pasta and zucchini and reduce heat to medium. Cook until the pasta and vegetables are tender, 13 to 15 minutes. Stir in the meatloaves and cook until heated through, 1 to 2 minutes.

3. Serving size: 1¾ cups

Chicken Sancocho

Total Time: 1:10 **Prep:** 0:20 **Cook:** 0:50 **Serves:** 6 **Difficulty:** Easy

This poultry version of the Latin American classic is chock full of hearty ingredients, including potatoes, yuca (also known as cassava), and plantains. Rich, meaty, bone-in chicken thighs simmer in the broth so they impart more flavor; after they're done, the meat gets shredded and stirred into the soup. Everyone gets to enjoy a large, deeply satisfying serving.

Ingredients

Olive oil — 4
1 Tbsp

Uncooked onion(s) — 0
1 medium, chopped

Garlic — 0
6 large clove(s), minced

Fresh tomato(es) — 0
1 cup(s), chopped

Ground cumin — 0
1 tsp

No-salt-added chicken stock — 2
6 cup(s)

Kosher salt — 0
1 ½ tsp

Uncooked yuca — 15
1 ½ cup(s), fresh or frozen, peeled and cut into bite-sized pieces

Uncooked red potato(es) — 6
¾ pound(s), baby variety, halved (or quartered if large)

Uncooked plantain(s) — 8
1 medium, green, peeled and cut into bite-sized pieces

Uncooked bone in skinless chicken thigh(s) — 19
1 ¾ pound(s)

Cilantro — 0
¾ cup(s)

Fresh yellow corn — 0
3 medium, each cut into 4 pieces

Instructions

1. Heat the oil in a Dutch oven over medium. Add the onion and garlic; cook until softened, about 5 minutes, stirring occasionally. Add the tomatoes and cumin; cook 1 minute, stirring frequently. Stir in the chicken stock, salt, yuca, potatoes, and plantain; bring to a boil over high heat. Add the chicken; cover, reduce the heat to low, and simmer until the chicken is done and the vegetables are tender, about 30 minutes.

2. Remove the chicken from the pot; cool slightly. Add ½ cup cilantro and corn to the pot; cook until the corn is crisp-tender, 7 to 8 minutes. Pull the chicken meat from the bones; discard the bones. Shred the chicken and stir into the soup. Sprinkle with the remaining ¼ cup cilantro.

3. Serving size: about 2 cups

Slow cooker chicken taco soup 4

Total Time: 6:05 **Prep:** 0:05 **Cook:** 6:00 **Serves:** 6 **Difficulty:** Easy

Slow cooker recipes that require lots of prep (tons of chopping and/or browning or sautéing) undermine the convenience promised by the appliance. So this recipe delivers ultimate ease with no chopping or browning—just stir everything together in the cooker (no need to thaw the veggies) and let it go. At the end, you'll shred the chicken, which takes almost no time.

Ingredients

Frozen corn kernels — 0
2 cup(s)

Frozen pepper strips — 0
1 ½ cup(s)

Frozen chopped onions — 0
⅔ cup(s)

Chili powder — 1
2 Tbsp

Ground cumin — 0
1 Tbsp

Garlic powder — 1
1 Tbsp

Table salt — 0
½ tsp

Salsa tatemada (roasted tomato salsa) — 1
16 oz

Canned kidney beans — 0
15 oz, rinsed and drained

Uncooked boneless skinless chicken thigh(s) — 17
1 ½ pound(s)

Shredded reduced-fat Mexican-style cheese — 5
6 Tbsp

Cilantro — 0
2 Tbsp, leaves (optional)

Instructions

1. In a slow cooker, combine the corn, pepper strips, onions, chili powder, cumin, garlic, salt, salsa, and beans. Stir in 2 cups water and the chicken thighs. Cover and cook on Low until the chicken is very tender, 6 to 7 hours.

2. Remove the chicken from the slow cooker; shred the meat with 2 forks and stir back into the soup. Ladle the soup into bowls; top with the cheese and cilantro, if desired.

3. Serving size: 1 ⅔ cups

Beef Soup with Potatoes & Carrots

7

Total Time: 0:45 **Prep:** 0:15 **Cook:** 0:30 **Serves:** 4 **Difficulty:** Easy

A couple of special touches turns this easy meat-and-potatoes (and carrots) soup into a memorable dish. Lots of sliced leeks lend a savory background note and become silky after simmering. Paprika is the main spice and can take the soup into whatever direction you prefer: Use regular paprika for a mild soup, hot Hungarian paprika for a spicy dish, or smoked paprika for woodsy essence.

Ingredients

Olive oil — 4
1 Tbsp

Uncooked 90% lean ground beef — 17
12 oz

Kosher salt — 0
1 tsp

Paprika — 0
1 tsp

Black pepper — 0
¾ tsp, divided

Unsalted beef stock — 1
2 ½ cup(s)

Uncooked leek(s) — 0
2 cup(s), thinly sliced

Uncooked russet potato — 7
12 oz, peeled and cut into chunks

Uncooked carrot(s) — 0
2 large, cut into chunks

Canned diced tomatoes — 0
14 ½ oz

Fresh parsley — 0
2 Tbsp, chopped

Instructions

1. Heat the oil in a Dutch oven over medium-high. Add the beef, salt, paprika, and ½ tsp black pepper; cook until the beef is browned, 5 to 6 minutes, stirring frequently to crumble. Stir in the beef stock, leeks, potatoes, carrots, and tomatoes; bring to a boil. Cover, reduce the heat to medium-low, and simmer until the vegetables are tender, 15 to 20 minutes. Sprinkle with the parsley and remaining ¼ tsp black pepper.

2. Serving size: 1 ¾ cups

Ajiaco (Colombian Chicken & Potato Stew)

Total Time: 1:10 **Prep:** 0:20 **Cook:** 0:50 **Serves:** 6 **Difficulty:** Easy

This classic South American soup is a hearty mix of gently poached chicken, different kinds of potatoes, corn on the cob (cut into manageable pieces), and a savory broth; garnishes always include crema (or sour cream) and capers. Traditionally, an herb called guascas flavors the broth, but we substitute easy-to-find dried oregano for a similar taste.

Ingredients

- Olive oil — 1 Tbsp — 4
- Uncooked onion(s) — 1 large, chopped — 0
- Garlic — 4 large clove(s), minced — 0
- No-salt-added chicken stock — 5 cup(s) — 1
- Uncooked Yukon gold potato(es) — ¾ pound(s), peeled and cut into bite-sized chunks — 5
- Uncooked red potato(es) — ¾ pound(s), halved (or quartered if large) — 6
- Dried oregano — 2 tsp — 0
- Kosher salt — 1 ½ tsp — 0
- Cilantro — 8 sprig(s), stems only — 0
- Uncooked skinless chicken breast with bone — 1 ¾ pound(s) — 0
- Uncooked sweet yellow corn — 2 ear(s), medium, each cut into 3 pieces — 0
- Mexican crema — 6 Tbsp — 10
- Avocado — 1 medium, thinly sliced — 8
- Capers — 2 Tbsp — 0
- Cilantro — 6 Tbsp, coarsely chopped — 0

Instructions

1. Heat the oil in a Dutch oven over medium. Add the onion and garlic; cook until softened, about 5 minutes, stirring occasionally. Add the chicken stock, potatoes, oregano, salt, and cilantro stems; bring to a boil over high heat. Add the chicken; cover, reduce the heat to low, and simmer until the chicken is done and the potatoes are tender, about 30 minutes.

2. Remove the chicken from the pot; cool slightly. Add the corn to the pot; cook until crisp-tender, 7 to 8 minutes. Pull the chicken meat from the bones; discard the bones. Shred the chicken and stir into the soup. Ladle 1 ⅓ cups soup into each of 6 bowls; top each serving with 1 tbsp crema, a few avocado slices, and 1 tsp each capers and cilantro.

3. Serving size: 1 1/2 cups

Printed in Great Britain
by Amazon